Y0-BYB-902

ONTOLOGY AND THE ART OF TRAGEDY

AN APPROACH TO ARISTOTLE'S *POETICS*

Martha Husain

State University of New York Press

Published by
State University of New York Press, Albany

© 2002 State University of New York

All rights reserved

Printed in the United States of America

No part of this book may be used or reproduced in any manner
whatsoever without written permission. No part of this
book may be stored in a retrieval system or transmitted
in any form or by any means including electronic,
electrostatic, magnetic tape, mechanical, photocopying,
recording, or otherwise without the prior permission in
writing of the publisher.

For information, address the State University of New York Press,
90 State Street, Suite 700, Albany, NY 12207

Production by Kelli Williams
Marketing by Patrick Durocher

Library of Congress Cataloging-in-Publication Data

Husain, Martha, 1937–
    Ontology and the art of tragedy: an approach to Aristotle's Poetics
Martha Husain.
        p. cm. — (SUNY series in ancient Greek philosophy)
    Includes bibliographical references and indexes.
    ISBN 0-7914-5143-7 (alk. paper). — ISBN 0-7914-5144-5 (pbk. : alk. paper)
    1. Aristotle. Poetics. 2. Tragedy. I. Title. II. Series.

PN1040.A53 H8734 2001
808.2—dc21   2001049302

10 9 8 7 6 5 4 3 2 1

SHATFORD LIBRARY

AUG   2002

PASADENA CITY COLLEGE
1570 E. COLORADO BLVD
PASADENA, CA 91106

CONTENTS

WITHDRAWN

PREFACE

The idea from which this study developed was suggested by my sister, Herta Schmid of the University of Berlin, in 1987. The Deutsche Akademische Austauschdienst supported it by a grant in 1988/89. Its final form took shape during a delightful sabbatical stay as a Visiting Fellow at the Australian National University in 1997.

The focus on questions of approach crystallized slowly, aided by teaching and the thinking of students, by giving and hearing papers at conferences and university colloquia, and by discussion and the teaching of joint courses with my colleague Murray Miles at Brock University. I am indebted to many scholars both for points on which I agree and for points on which I disagree with them. One's debts *legetai pollachos.*

A word on texts, translation, and secondary literature may not be out of place here.

I have in general relied on the Oxford Classical Texts, and for the *Metaphysics* in particular on Ross's corrected 1953 Oxford Clarendon edition. For the *Poetics* I have relied on Kassel's 1965 Oxford Classical Texts edition. This has been used in conjunction with Lucas's 1968 commented edition of the text and with Halliwell's 1987 commented translation. Both have recorded few disagreements with Kassel's text, most of which do not affect the argument. Lucas had adopted Kassel's text, noting that the few places where he would have preferred a different reading are "negligible" (v). Halliwell lists his divergences from Kassel (66–68 of his Textual Notes), but only one really bears on the argument. There is thus an up-to-date reliable text available, which supersedes earlier editions. Other editions and commentaries have been consulted on contentious issues.[1]

My translations generally follow the Oxford Translation, to which I wish to record my indebtedness. I have, however, changed it in the light of other translations and commentaries and of the following principles: I have rendered *einai* as "to be" rather than as "to exist," deleted all

vii

PREFACE

emphases and capitalizations that are not based on the text, deleted single quotations marks where they seemed misleading, and frequently sacrificed elegance for literalness. For the *Poetics* I have followed Halliwell's splendidly readable commented translation of 1987, though with changes where I felt them to be appropriate.

As for secondary literature, there is so much of it, by so many scholars in different fields, that an exhaustive survey would be impossible in what is meant to be a reasonably small book. This inevitably leaves some works out that deserve mention and makes the consideration of others too brief to do justice to their complexity. For both my apologies.

I thank my colleague Murray Miles for reading the text in its entirety and greatly improving its readability. And my gratitude to Irene Cherrington, the departmental secretary, is great in this as in many other things. I also wish to acknowledge the generosity of the Classics Department at Brock University, which has made its resources and expertise available to me for many years. My special thanks go to Fred Casler who first taught me Greek and to Richard Parker who read the *Poetics* in Greek with Murray Miles and me. The book also owes significant improvements to the fine work of my research assistant, Stefan Rodde.

The following list of italicized transliterated Greek terms, with translations, is to serve for the reader's orientation. These are technical terms that recur frequently. Keeping them in this form highlights how technical and consistent Aristotle's language in the *Poetics* is. But when any of these terms occur in longer Greek quotes, they are given in Greek script.

aitia or *aition*	cause, reason
aporia (aporiai, aporetic)	difficulty
arche (archai)	principle, beginning
ousia (ousiai)	substance
dia (mostly used as *di'*)	through, because
dianoia	articulated rationality
dynamis	potentiality
ethos (ethe)	moral character
eidos (eide)	form, formal cause
einai (on, onta, esti)	to be
eleeinon (eleos)	pitiful
energeia	actuality
episteme (epistemai)	science
ergon	work, function
hyle	matter, material cause
katharsis (katharon)	clarification
lexis	language, delivery

logos (logoi)	language, speech, account, definition
melopoiia	choral lyrics
meros (mere)	part
mimesis (mimeseis, mimetic, mimetes)	imitation
mythos (mythoi)	plot-structure, story
oikeion	integral, of one's household
opsis	spectacle
pathos (pathema, pathemata)	action, event, emotion
perainein (perainousa)	to achieve, to complete
peri hena	focused on one person
peri mian praxin	focused on one action
poiesis (poiein, poietes, poietike)	making, poetry
praxis (praktike)	action
pros (pros ti, pros hen, pros ta theatra)	in relation to
phoberon (phobos)	fearsome
physis	nature
psyche	soul
rhetor (rhetorike)	public speaker
synthesis or *systasis*	structure
synolon (synola)	a composite being
techne (technai, technites)	craft
telos (tele, telic, auto-telic, hetero-telic)	end, purpose, final cause
tragikon (tragodia)	tragic

INTRODUCTION

This study is not a new translation nor primarily a new exegesis of the *Poetics* but a sustained reflection on the principles and criteria that should guide an approach to this text. It aims at developing a canon for establishment, translation, and exegesis of the text. Since these three aspects of its reception are interconnected rather than neatly sequential, all three must be guided by the same principles and criteria.

Such reflections are of course always present, at least implicitly, in scholarly attempts at reception of this as of any other ancient Greek text. For reception is beset by so many difficulties that it cannot be achieved unreflectively. The difficulties are of two kinds. First, the ambiguity of the ancient texts themselves makes reception governed by different principles and criteria defensible. The ambiguity results in large part from the loss of context. For in their own time they stood in a concrete context within which their meaning could be ascertained by recourse to a much richer and denser environment consisting of other Aristotelian texts, of those of other philosophers and schools, of the literary and wider culture around them, of the historical sources, and even of the author and his colleagues and students as also of his rivals and opponents. The second difficulty arises from our own historical situation in the long and varied history of exegesis. The texts have been filtered through different layers of the vagaries of transmission, of translation, and of interpretation in terms of later purposes, conceptual frameworks, and methodological approaches. These later purposes, conceptual frameworks, and methodological approaches are enormously diverse and affect not only our ability to get back to the ancient texts themselves but even our willingness to make the attempt. Aristotle's *Poetics* in particular has been appropriated in such diverse ways that access to the text itself has been obscured.

In the face of these difficulties, the present study attempts to develop principles and criteria for reception of the text itself. For while its diverse appropriations may be legitimate and worthwhile within their own parameters, both intellectual honesty and the furtherance of critical scholarly debate would seem to demand that those parameters be delineated in careful reflection, so that they can be assessed both in terms of their power to illumine the text and in their limitations. The here proposed principles and criteria are meant to be a contribution to such reflection and debate.

My guiding heuristic principle is von Trendelenburg's celebrated dictum: *Aristoteles ex Aristotele*. This can never be more than a guiding principle, since one cannot leave one's historical situation and magically return to Aristotle's Lyceum. But it can also never be less, if the attempt to understand the text in and for itself is not to be abandoned. And that attempt, notwithstanding all the difficulties, is worth preserving, not only for the text's intrinsic interest and value and the preservation of our intellectual heritage, but also as the indispensable precondition of understanding what it is that we are appropriating in terms of diverse purposes, conceptual frameworks, and methodological approaches.

At this point it is reasonable to ask why one should concern oneself with developing a canon for the reception of the *Poetics* in particular rather than for Aristotle's works as a whole. For surely the *Poetics*, as a small and incomplete part of that whole, cannot be understood apart from it. This is true, but two considerations mandate the development of principles and criteria for this text in particular. One is the nature of an individual Aristotelian treatise, the other its particular location within the *corpus* as a whole. An individual treatise has a distinct subject matter of its own, which it elucidates in terms of substantive-methodological *archai* of its own. This substantive-methodological differentiation is made possible by the flexibility of Aristotle's technical vocabulary. While certain key concepts apply to all his works and stamp them as Aristotelian, they nevertheless function differently within different subject matters. *An. Post.* I. 76a37–40 even characterizes the common basic truths of demonstrative science as analogous rather than identical for different sciences. Such differences must be taken into account, if reception of any individual treatise is to be achieved. Secondly, an individual treatise has a particular location within the *corpus* as a whole in the sense that the network of its relationships with the other treatises is unique. It may need to be read to a greater or lesser extent in the light of others, and the achievement of reception hinges crucially on identifying those other treatises correctly. This is especially important for a small and incomplete text such as the *Poetics*.

The present study is motivated in part by the belief that the *Poetics* has not always been understood as having a distinctive subject matter of its own, and that it has all too often been read in the light of the wrong other treatises. This has obscured both how technical Aristotle's vocabulary is and how it functions in this text. The reason for this study is therefore also partly polemical. The study embodies a proposal to read the *Poetics* as having a distinctive subject matter of its own, whose location in the *corpus* is such that it should be read principally in the light of the *Metaphysics* rather than of the *Ethics-Politics* or *Rhetoric*.[1] Whether this proposal turns out to be right or wrong or somewhere in between, it is perhaps worthwhile to work it out and to present it as an alternative and as a contribution to the critical scholarly debate on the metalevel, at which alone principles and criteria for reception can be refined in such a way as to achieve a better approximation to von Trendelenburg's guiding heuristic principle.

The basic idea of the present approach, namely, to read the *Poetics ex Aristotele* in the context of his philosophy, is not new. Frede (in Rorty 1992), and Belfiore 1992 have clearly expressed this as a desideratum, as have other scholars earlier. In fact, all responsible classical scholarship attempts this.

What is new is rather the deliberate, sustained, systematic, and sequential focus on questions of approach. Its purpose is to give the adjective *Aristotelian* conceptual content by making the author's understanding of Aristotle's philosophy explicit. For it is only by giving conceptual content to the adjective *Aristotelian* that what the author means by reading the *Poetics* as an *Aristotelian* treatise can be made clear—and only this can in turn subject that meaning to critical debate. The four chapters bring the conceptual content of *Aristotelian* to bear on the *Poetics*.

Chapter 1 sets out the author's approach to the *corpus* as a systematic doctrinal whole, marked as Aristotelian by a core of pervasive substantive-methodological conceptual constants. These are: the concept of being, the categories of being, the categorial priority of *ousia*, immanent causal form-matter constitution in the category of *ousia*, and the ontological and cognitive priority of the object. These comprise Aristotle's distinctive philosophy of being, as primarily elucidated in the *Metaphysics*. The *Poetics* is to be read in this context.

Chapter 2 locates the subject matter of the *Poetics* within this distinctive philosophy of being by gradual adumbration, successively narrowing it down from the full extension of being *(panta ta onta)*, through the craft-nature disjunction, the artistic craft–useful craft disjunction, the literary arts–visual arts disjunction, to the tragic literary art.

Chapter 3 shows that Aristotle conceptualizes a tragedy in terms of his distinctive philosophy of being, because the pervasive substantive-methodological conceptual constants are either explicitly or implicitly present in the text of the *Poetics*. The chapter distinguishes and evaluates different kinds of direct and indirect textual evidence and concludes that Aristotle understands a tragedy as a *synolon*, a composite being in the category of *ousia*, with all that that entails for him.

Chapter 4 contrasts tragic, ethical, and rhetorical action in terms of the *synolon*, on which each one is centered. Tragic action in the *Poetics* is object-centered on the tragedy, ethical action in the *Nicomachean Ethics* is agent-centered on the ethical agent, rhetorical action in the *Rhetoric* is patient-centered on the audience. The three modes of centering are mutually exclusive, from which it follows that the *Poetics* cannot be read either in the light of the *Ethics* or of the *Rhetoric*. It must instead be read in the light of the *Metaphysics*, which sets out the object-centered structure of natural and man-made *ousiai*.

The *Appendix* deals with textual evidence, particularly with the distinction between the lexical and the textual meaning of the technical vocabulary of the *Poetics*. It makes some recommendations for translation, and it shows that the approach of the present study can resolve exegetical difficulties that arise from other approaches.

A new exegesis of the *Poetics* emerges from this approach. Since the latter has been made explicit, its link with the exegesis is clarified. Clarification of the link between approach and exegesis is one of the purposes of the present study.

The most important and perhaps surprising features of the new exegesis are as follows: Aristotle's *Poetics* is well integrated into, and consistent with, his distinctive philosophy of being. A tragedy is categorized and defined as an *ousia* with an intrinsic definitory nature of its own, hence *katharsis* in the formal definition cannot be in the tertiary category of *pros ti*. Two distinct *mimetic* levels (*mimesis* 1 and *mimesis* 2, respectively) connect a tragedy with nature and with human life. The tragic *(to tragikon)* is art-specific for Aristotle, it is the specific nature of a tragedy *(tragike mimesis)*, and the *mythos* functions as its compositional principle or "soul."

The final assessment of his theory of art sees its strength and continuing relevance in the antireductionist conceptual elucidation of the adjective *artistic*, a feat rarely equalled in the 2,300 years since Aristotle. It sees its weakness in its representational tie with human life, which renders it unable to encompass nonrepresentational art.

The present study's emphasis on questions of approach makes it possible to put scholarly debates on a more fundamental level. For example, Belfiore 1992, chapter 8, sees the fundamental exegetical contrast between the intrinsic and the homeopathic interpretations of *katharsis*. She proposes an allopathic view as the fundamental contrast to the homeopathic. But bringing Aristotle's distinctive philosophy of being to bear on the issue, shows both the homeopathic and the allopathic views to be but variants of patient-centering. The fundamental distinction is between patient-centering and object-centering, which is for Aristotle a sharp and mutually exclusive divide. Only when his three modes of centering with their normal Aristotelian implications are taken into account, do the *Poetics* and *Ethics* and *Rhetoric* become comparable, and only then can the location of the *Poetics* within the *corpus* be assessed.

The project of reading the *Poetics* in light of the *Metaphysics* necessitates a preliminary (chapter 1) presentation of Aristotle's distinctive philosophy of being. This is indispensable as it introduces the reader to the basic concepts of Aristotle's thought-world, and so to the conceptual space within which the *Poetics* is located. If the *Poetics* is to be understood as an Aristotelian treatise, an awareness of these concepts is necessary.

Chapter 1

APPROACH TO THE *CORPUS* AS A WHOLE

1.1 The Systematic, the Chronological, the Aporetic Approach

One's approach to any individual treatise presupposes an approach to the *corpus* as a whole, which should be made clear at the beginning. For scholars have understood Aristotle's works, and so have understood what "Aristotelian" means, in different ways. The three main approaches have been the systematic, the chronological, and the *aporetic*. The systematic approach holds that all parts of the whole stand in ascertainable doctrinal relationships, which consist of pervasive substantive-methodological conceptual constants. The latter enable one to understand the works as a body of positive Aristotelian philosophy, which is not a mere aggregate of unconnected treatises but an understandable doctrinal plurality in unity. Scholars differ, however, on what those pervasive conceptual constants are, and so on what the positive philosophy is. The chronological approach holds that all parts of the whole stand in ascertainable chronological relationships of simultaneity and of earlier and later date. Chronology is usually linked with the notion of development, thus enabling one to understand the works as the record of Aristotle's philosophical development. The works are not a mere aggregate of unconnected treatises but an understandable developmental plurality in unity. Scholars differ, however, as to the *terminus a quo* and the *terminus ad quem* of this development, and so as to what its nature and dynamics are. The *aporetic* approach has not been developed for the *corpus* as a whole but rather for individual treatises or parts of such treatises, particularly the *Metaphysics*. It is therefore not a holistic approach comparable to the other two, but it is distinct from them because it interprets treatises or parts of treatises considered *aporetic* not in terms of a positive doctrinal content or of a positive developmental stage. Whether it is capable of understanding the *corpus* as more than a mere aggregate of unconnected treatises seems doubtful.[1]

A choice among these three basic approaches cannot be avoided. They specify the most general parameters within which scholars must try to ascertain the meaning of the *corpus* as a whole and so of any individual treatise. Within each of these parameters, further choices must be made as to the nature of the doctrinal content, the nature and stages of Aristotle's philosophical development, and the nature and function of *aporiai*. These choices must of course be argued. They normally grow out of and become explicit as a crystallization of a scholar's personal engagement with the text. For the purposes of this study, I should like to present my own choices with a minimum of supporting argument. They can perhaps be accepted as hypotheses to be tested in terms of both their power and their limitations in illumining the *Poetics*.

My basic choice among the three main approaches is the systematic. This does not mean that I reject the other two in the sense of holding that individual treatises do not stand in chronological and developmental relationships, or that no parts of treatises are *aporetic*. It means rather that I consider the systematic approach to be presupposed by the other two. For the notion of development is not purely chronological but involves a substantive, indeed a doctrinal, content. The *terminus a quo* and the *terminus ad quem* are not mere dates but positive philosophical positions. One needs a positive doctrinal notion of Aristotelian philosophy before one can map out its developmental direction and stages. Likewise, the *aporetic* approach presupposes a doctrinal context within which *aporiai* have significance and function. Aristotle makes this clear when he argues for an important but limited and preliminary function of *aporiai* at *Met.* III. 995a24–b4. Scholars have acknowledged this, and nobody to my knowledge has ever argued that his works are nothing but *aporetic,* or that *aporiai* are stated purely for their own sake. I suspect that such a notion would not only conflict with Aristotle's own assessment of the role of *aporiai* in his philosophy, but would be inherently senseless. *Aporiai* cannot arise in a vacuum; they are prompted by specific difficulties that are embedded in a doctrinal context from which they derive their significance and possibility of resolution.

1.2 The Pervasive Substantive-Methodological Conceptual Constants

My basic choice therefore is to approach the *corpus* systematically in terms of an ascertainable doctrinal content, which is common to all the treatises but whose different aspects are developed in individual ones. The common core consists of pervasive substantive-methodological conceptual constants which, however, function somewhat differently in different treatises. It is this common core that specifies what "Aristotelian" means to me. Yet the systematic plurality in unity of his works is unlike modern models. The constants are both substantive and methodological at once, since Aristotle does not have our notion of a mere method nor that of the priority of method to subject matter. Method is not only adapted to, but determined by, the nature of the subject matter. Aristotle's word *method (methodos)* contains the noun *path (hodos)* and so suggests one's walking along a path that takes one from somewhere definite to somewhere else definite and is shaped by the contours of the landscape over which it winds. Cognition is both systematic *(hodoi)* and veridical *(alethes)*, because method is adapted to subject matter rather than the other way round. That is why Aristotle most generally characterizes method as a progression from what is better known to us to what is more knowable by nature, where both *termini* are aspects of the objective being of things. For things are both perceptible *(aistheta)* and intelligible *(noeta)* in their own being. At *E.N.* I. 3, Aristotle excoriates the inappropriate transfer of method from one subject matter to another as a want of culture. The priority of subject matter to method is one aspect of the ontological and cognitive priority *(proteron)* of the object to the subject.[2] As a result, Aristotle's technical vocabulary is flexible rather than rigidly univocal, so that the conceptual constants can function somewhat differently in different treatises while yet preserving a distinctively Aristotelian texture and meaning.

Within the systematic approach, my choice of the pervasive substantive-methodological conceptual constants comprises those which I hold to be explicitly or implicitly present and foundational in all his treatises. They are explicitly present when they are stated in so many words in a text, implicitly when they are not so stated but used. They are explicitly foundational when they are said to be so, implicitly when they are not said to be so but used. Their presence and importance cannot be explicit in every treatise, since each has a distinctive subject matter of its own and since the *corpus* would otherwise largely consist of endless repetition. The constants must therefore be ascertained by reference to completely general statements, which identify them as common to, and foundational for, all things. Their implicit presence and importance in a given treatise must be confirmed by indications of their use. One's choice of constants on this dual basis is always open to debate.

I choose the following conceptual constants (again with a minimum of supporting argument), by reference to completely general statements in the *Metaphysics*, while postponing until chapter 3 their confirmation by reference to indications of their use in the *Poetics:* the concept of being, the categories of being, the categorial priority of *ousia,* immanent causal form-matter constitution in the category of *ousia,* and the ontological and cognitive priority of the object.[3]

1.2.1 The Concept of Being

The concept of being is common to and foundational for all things, because Aristotle understands philosophy to have the question "What is being?" at its core: "And indeed the question which was raised of old and is raised now and always and is always the subject of doubt, 'What is being?'" (*Met.* VII. 1028b2–4). The deliberate combination of "of old" *(palai),* "now" *(nyn),* and "always" *(aei)* indicates that Aristotle not only ranks himself as a philosopher of being in the tradition of Parmenides and Plato, but that he considers philosophy's central concern with being ("what is being?" *ti to on*) as holding true for all time. The "always" goes in its assertion of unchangeable core importance far beyond Homer's formula, which combines past, present, and future tense *(en, estin, estai).* While Aristotle realizes that the earliest philosophers were concerned more with becoming than with being, he does not interpret this as meaning that philosophy of becoming is an alternative to philosophy of being, but rather that early philosophy must be forgiven for its as yet inadequate grasp of its subject: "For the earliest philosophy is, on all subjects, like one who lisps, since it is young and in its beginnings" (*Met.* I. 993a15–16). Aristotle explicitly restates that being is a truly pervasive conceptual constant, e.g., "and being is common to all things" *(koinon de pasi to on estin; Met.* IV. 1004b20). The "common" *(koinon)* echoes Heraclitus's earlier statement: "But the *logos* is common" *(tou logou d'eontos xynou;* Diels-Kranz, Frg. 2, lns. 2–3) and, like it, is unrestricted in its generality. Being pertains to all things without exception *(pasi).* Its equally unrestricted foundational importance is reflected in Aristotle's technical vocabulary, which designates all things as beings *(onta),* collectively as all beings *(panta ta onta)* and individually as a being *(on).* From an earlier colloquial meaning as things in general and as property or possessions in particular, beings *(onta)* was elevated to the role of the core technical philosophical concept by Parmenides (in the singular *to on*) and by Plato (in the singular and plural *to on* and *ta onta*). It is so retained by Aristotle. Philosophical conceptualization attains a proper grasp on reality only on the ground of being, for the concept of being comprises all things in its extension. To fall outside that extension is not to be at all, to have no mode of being whatsoever.

1.2.2 The Categories of Being

But being is not a univocal concept. It is common to all things not univocally *(kath hen)* but in categorially differentiated focal meaning *(pros hen)*.[4] This distinctively Aristotelian understanding of being is not only his first line of defense against the undifferentiated unity of Parmenidean being but, even more importantly, enables him to preserve the richly differentiated yet ordered being of things while conceptualizing them in terms of one pervasive core concept. The understanding of being in terms of the *pros hen* focused categories of being is inseparable from that pervasive core concept itself. The categorial *pros hen* structure is as unrestrictedly general and foundational as being itself. "Being is spoken in many senses" *(to on legetai pollachos)* is Aristotle's metaphysical *Leitmotif,* repeated in many treatises explicitly or implicitly. In a rare display of one-upmanship over his colleagues in the Academy, who still rely on Plato's *Sophist* to counter the threat of the Parmenidean univocity of being, he sets his understanding of being off against their antiquated *(archaïkos)* views:

> [T]hey framed the difficulty in an obsolete form. For they thought that all things that are would be one *(viz.* Being itself), if one did not join issue with and refute the saying of Parmenides: "For never will this be proved, that things that are not are." They thought it necessary to prove that that which is not is; for only thus—of that which is and something else—could the things that are be composed, if they are many. ... But it is absurd, or rather impossible, that the coming into play of a single thing should bring it about that part of that which is is a this *(tode),* part a such *(toionde),* part a so much *(tosonde),* part a here *(pou).* (*Met.* XIV. 1089a1–15)

The strong language of "absurd" *(atopon)* and "impossible" *(adynaton)* is echoed in many other places, where Aristotle argues that the categorial understanding of being must precede the quest for the causal *archai* and elements of being. To give but one example: "In general, if we search for the elements of beings without distinguishing the many senses in which things are said to be, we cannot find them . . . but if the elements can be discovered at all, it is only the elements of *ousiai"* (*Met.* I. 992b18–22).[5]

1.2.3 *The Categorial Priority of* Ousia

The ontological and cognitive priority of *ousia* is implicit in this structure, for *ousia* is the focal meaning, the *pros hen* reference, of all the other categories. In the same context in which Aristotle identifies being as the perennially valid core concept of philosophy, he immediately, actually in the same sentence, goes on to reformulate the question "What is being?" *(ti to on)* as paradigmatically meaning "What is *ousia*?" *(tis he ousia):* "And indeed the question which was raised of old and is raised now and always and is always the subject of doubt, 'What is being?' is the question 'What is *ousia*?' " (*Met.* VII. 1028b2–4). He credits his predecessors with having had at least an inkling of this truth, since all of them really sought the causal *archai* and elements of *ousiai,* however vaguely: "For it is this that some assert to be one, others more than one, and that some assert to be limited in number, others unlimited" (*Met.* VII. 1028b4–6). He places himself within this tradition: "And so we also must consider chiefly and primarily and so to say exclusively what that is which is in this sense" (*Met.* VII. 1028b6–7).

The reformulation of the question is carefully modified in the text, so as to make clear that it is not meant to be reductive. Reformulating the question "What is being?" as "What is *ousia*?" does not reduce being to *ousia* or shrink the extension of being; nor does it deny the legitimacy of conceptualizing all things in all categories as being. Indeed, reduction would destroy the status of the categories as categories of being *(kategoriai tou ontos)* together with their *pros hen* structure. *Ousia* enjoys categorial priority in the sense that it functions as *pros hen* focus, not in the sense that it absorbs all being into itself. All other categories are understood as different secondary categorial modes of the being of individual *ousiai.*[6]

The different dimensions of the functioning of *ousia* as *pros hen* focus are carefully set out: "Now there are several senses in which a thing is said to be first, yet *ousia* is first in every sense, in definition *(logoi),* in knowledge *(gnosei),* in time *(chronoi)*" (*Met.* VII. 1028a31–33). Translating *logoi* as "in definition" seems defensible, since the priority of *ousia* in definition *(horismos, horos, horos tes ousias)* is a central concern of the *Metaphysics.* The priority of *ousia* in definition means that definition pertains to *ousia* primarily, to the other categorial modes only secondarily: "But this is evident, that definition *(horismos)* and essence *(to ti en einai)* in the primary *(protos)* and unqualified *(haplos)* sense belong to *ousiai*; still they belong to the others as well but not in the primary sense" (*Met.* VII. 1030b4–7). Definition follows the categorial *pros hen* structure of being, because it is the formula *(logos)* of the essence *(to ti en einai)* and of the what a thing is *(to ti estin)*, and these too follow that structure: "[E]ssence will likewise belong in the primary and unqualified sense to *ousia* and in a secondary sense *(eita)* to the other categories, as will the what a thing is, not essence in the unqualified sense but essence as belonging to quality or quantity . . . by virtue of reference *(pros)* to one and the same thing . . . not with a single meaning *(kath hen)* but by focal reference *(pros hen)*" *(Met.* VII. 1030a29–b3). Focal reference means that "in the definition of each secondary categorial mode that of its *ousia* must be present *(ananke enyparchein)*" *(Met.* VII. 1028a35–36; cf. IX. 1045b26–32). *Ousia,* then, functions as a component in the definition of each one of its secondary categorial modes of being.

This entails that it is prior in knowledge *(gnosei)* because "we think that we know *(eidenai)* each thing most *(malista)* when we know *(gnomen)* what a man or fire is *(ti estin)*, rather than its quality, its quantity, or its place" *(Met.* VII. 1028a36–b1). Since the definition of an *ousia* must be present in that of each of its secondary categorial modes, only *ousia* can be understood independently and intrinsically in its own category (intracategorially), while each of the other categories must be understood dependently by *pros hen* reference to *ousia* (intercategorially).

The lack of cognitive independence of the secondary categorial modes of being is due to their lack of ontological independence. *Ousia* is prior in time *(chronoi),* which entails its separate being: "For of the other categories none is separate *(choriston)* but only *ousia*" *(Met.* VII. 1028a33–34). Since cognition is for Aristotle veridical and grasps being as it is, "as each thing is in respect of being, so it is in respect of truth" *(Met.* II. 993b30–31), a categorial mode that cannot be separately on its own, can also not be so understood. The most fundamental and most often repeated contrast between *ousia* and the secondary categories is that only the former has independent being while the latter are hung up on it *(eretai).* E.g., "The substratum *(hypokeimenon)* is *ousia,* and this is in one sense the matter *(hyle)* . . . and in another sense the definition and form *(logos kai morphe)* . . . and in a third sense the compound of these, which alone . . . is unqualifiedly separate *(choriston haplos)*" *(Met.* VIII. 1042a26–31). Priority in *ousia* means surpassing *(hyperballein)* the other categorial modes in being when separated *(chorizomena toi einai)* *(Met.* XIII. 1077b2–3). Being *choriston* or *chorizomenon* means priority in respect of nature and *ousia* *(kata physin kai ousian)* such that *ousia* "can be without the others, while they cannot be without *(aneu)* it" *(Met.* V. 1019a2–4). For each of the other categorial modes is dependent on *ousia* for its very being: "Clearly then it is through *(dia)* this category that each of the others also is" *(Met.* VII. 1028a29–30). This real dependence is linguistically reflected in the adjectival form of properties in the secondary categories *(paronymy),* for which

Aristotle argues and which he justifies in *Met.* IX. 7, even coining a new technical term, "thaten" *(ekeininon).* It emphasizes the dependent being and intelligibility of all the secondary categorial modes, even if a verb rather than an adjective with *esti* is used (cf. *Met.* VII. 1028a20–31).

1.2.4 Immanent Causal Form-Matter Constitution in the Category of Ousia

The reason for this real and cognitive priority of *ousia* is that it alone is causally constituted by form and matter. The secondary categorial modes have form but no matter, since the composite *ousia* serves as their real and predicative substratum and subject: "Nor does matter *(hyle)* belong to all those things which are by nature *(physei)* but are not *ousiai,* but their substratum *(hypokeimenon)* is the *ousia*" (*Met.* VIII. 1044b8–9; I. 992b21–22). Only an *ousia* is intracategorially (in its own category) constituted by form and matter, which are themselves *ousiai,* e.g., "There are three kinds of *ousia*—the matter *(hyle)* . . . the nature *(physis)* . . . and thirdly the individual *ousia* which is constituted out of these *(he ek touton),* for example, Socrates or Callias" (*Met.* XII. 1070a9–13; cf. VII. 1034b34–5a9). Self-constituting in its own category, an individual *ousia* is actualized and so defined by its immanent form: "[F]or the *ousia* is the indwelling form *(to eidos to enon),* from which and the matter the compound is called *ousia*" (*Met.* VII. 1037a29–30). Therefore, properties in the secondary categorial modes cannot enter constitutively and hence not definitionally into substantial being:

> And further it is impossible *(adynaton)* and absurd *(atopon)* for a this *(tode)* and *ousia,* if it is constituted of some things, not to be constituted of *ousiai* or of a definite this *(ek tou tode ti)* but of quality *(ek poiou).* For in that case what is not *ousia* but quality will be prior to the *ousia* and to the this. But this is impossible, for neither in definition nor in time nor in coming to be can the properties be prior to the *ousia,* for they will then also be separate. (*Met.* VII. 1038b23–29; cf. XIV. 1088b2–4)

Pros hen categorial structure is asymmetrical, grounded in the intracategorial immanent form-matter constitution of *ousia.*

That constitution accounts for the unity of substantial being. Aristotle's tone is nearly jubilant when he resolves the *aporia,* how a composite *ousia* can be one, by understanding form as actuality *(energeia)* and matter as potentiality *(dynamis):* "But, as has been said, the proximate matter and the form are one and the same thing, the one potentially and the other actually . . . for each thing is a definite unity *(hen gar ti),* and the potential and the actual are somehow one *(hen pos estin)* so that there is no other cause" (*Met*. VIII. 1045b17–22). *Met*. IX. 7 extends *paronymy* from properties in the secondary categories to the constitutive matter in the category of *ousia*, based on its relative (not absolute) indeterminacy *(aorista)*, which enables it to be determinable to the actualizing power of form as determinant. A determinate individual *ousia* results from this immanent causally constitutive functioning of determinable and determinant as *archai*. Since Aristotle announces this as his own solution to the *aporia* of substantial unity at the end of Book VIII, while IX. 7 simply works it out further, these passages can be accepted as doctrinal (unlike the more *aporetic* VII.7).[7]

The asymmetrical *pros hen* structure of the categories of being and the priority of *ousia* (which is grounded in its intracategorial form-matter constitution) are as general as being itself and inseparable from Aristotle's understanding of being:

> But the senses of being itself *(kath hauta de einai legetai)* are precisely as many as the figures of predication *(ta schemata tes kategorias)* signify; for the senses of being are just as many as they. Since then some of these signify what a thing is, some its quality, some its quantity, some relation, some doing or being affected, some place, some time, being in each of these signifies the same. (*Met*. V. 1017a22–27; cf. XII. 1070a31–b2; *Physics* III. 200b32–1a9)

This entire complex can, I believe, be accepted as a core conceptual constant. For not only has Aristotle equated being with it, at *Met*. IV. 1, 2, and 3 he also maps out the domains of all sciences *(epistemai)* within it. Metaphysical *episteme* investigates all beings *(panta ta onta)*, so that the unrestricted extension of being is its subject matter, which means that its method must be investigation *qua* being *(hei on)*. Each special *episteme* cuts off from *panta ta onta* a part *(meros)* and hence is partial *(en merei)*. Its subject matter is then a part of the extension of being, either a substantial genus such as the animal kingdom or a secondary categorial aspect of the being of things such as the quantitative. This determines its method to be investigation either *qua* a substantial generic nature such as animality or *qua* a secondary categorial what it is *(ti esti)* such as quantity.

1.2.5 The Ontological and Cognitive Priority of the Object

The ontological and cognitive priority of the object to the subject is clear in many contexts. Nowhere does Aristotle allow any subjective contribution to enter constitutively into the being of things. Truth is defined as correspondence: "It is not because we think that you are pale, that you are pale, but because you are pale we who say this have the truth" (*Met.* IX. 1051b6–9; cf. IV. 1011b23–29). Aristotle makes fun of the Protagorean priority of the subject to the object:

> We call both knowledge and perception the measure of things for the same reason, because we know something by them—while as a matter of fact they are measured rather than measure. . . . Protagoras says "man is the measure of all things". . . . Such thinkers are saying nothing while they seem to say something remarkable. (*Met.* X. 1053a31–b3)

Things are not measured by our knowledge—our knowledge is measured by things. Aristotle is an epistemological realist. That is why *De Anima* II.5–III.8 understands all modes of knowledge as deriving their cognitional content from the things themselves, so that the perceptible and intelligible forms in things and as received in the soul are the same. Thus the soul of man is cognitionally all things.[8]

The here chosen pervasive conceptual constants constitute Aristotle's distinctive philosophy of being and so the systematic framework within which I propose to approach the *Poetics*.

Chapter 2

APPROACH TO THE *POETICS*

2.1 The Poetics *as a Special Science*

My approach to the *Poetics* rests on the three beliefs that the above pervasive conceptual constants apply to it, that it is an individual Aristotelian treatise, and that it has a particular location within the *corpus*. No argument has been given by any scholar that Aristotle's distinctive understanding of being does not apply to this text, and there are indications of the use of all the constants in it. These I defer until chapter 3.[1] Its being an individual treatise means that it is not part of any other treatise but has a distinctive subject matter of its own, investigated in terms of substantive-methodological *archai* of its own. Its having a particular location within the *corpus* means that the network of its relationships with the other treatises is unique. My approach accepts the *Poetics* as a genuine special science *(episteme en merei)*.[2]

This presupposes that it is an *episteme*, a point that calls for some supporting argument. For *prima facie* it conflicts with Aristotle's care to free *episteme* from subservience to practical or productive ends (e.g., in *Met.* I), with his distinction between practical *(praktike)*, productive *(poietike)*, and theoretical *(theoretike)* discursive thinking *(dianoia)* (e.g., at *Met.* VI. 1025b25), and with the reconstructed title of the *Poetics* itself. For that title as it stands, *Aristotle's About the Poetical (Aristotelous peri poietikes)*, needs to be completed by supplying a noun, which the adjective *Poetical* can modify. This is, most reasonably, *Art (techne)* rather than *Science (episteme)*. Would Aristotle accept the *Poetics* as being an *episteme* rather than a *techne*?

I believe that he would. For his care to free *episteme* from subservience to practical or productive ends means that he distinguishes between *episteme* and *praxis* and *poiesis* in a manner that we would today express as the distinction between an object- and a metalevel. The entire *corpus* is philosophy, and each of its individual treatises is a philosophy of a subject matter. On the object-level this may be purely theoretical such as physics, or practical such as man's ethical life, or productive such as a *techne*. Yet, however practical or productive the subject matter may be, the philosopher's investigation of it is *epistemic* and has as its end theoretical understanding. This is indeed not subservient to the practical or productive ends that are part of its subject matter. Wonder, as the imperative that impels humans to philosophize, raises the desire to know above such subservience in all domains of being. The philosopher can study the practical or productive ends of a *praxis* or of a *techne* as objectively and disinterestedly as he can study the theoretical ones of physics or mathematics. Some terminological confusion arises for the modern reader because, in some contexts, Aristotle reserves *episteme* for demonstrative science, and because he uses it on both the meta- and the object-level in the case of theoretical sciences. But in the case of a *praxis* or a *poiesis* he usually (though not invariably) makes a terminological distinction, reserving *episteme* for the metalevel and using *praxis* and *techne* for the object-level (*techne* and *poiesis* are used interchangeably, see *E.N.* VI. 4). The title of the *Poetics* is therefore not *Aristotle's Poetical Techne (Aristotelous poietike techne)* but *Aristotle's About Poetical Techne (Aristotelous peri poietikes technes)*. The *About (peri)* indicates the theoretical and so *epistemic* metalevel. It follows that the *Poetics* is not a how-to book for aspiring playwrights or critics, for while some advice to these aspirants is included, it is marginal. Aristotle is not a consultant to professional associations.[3]

The claim that the *Poetics* is an individual Aristotelian treatise needs to be substantiated by delineating what I take its distinctive subject matter to be. That, however, can only be done by gradual adumbration, for it lies within a number of successively narrowing parts of the full extension of being *(panta ta onta)*. These must be taken into account in order to understand both the treatise's subject matter and its location within the *corpus*.

2.2 Techne-Physis (Mimesis 1)

The first and most general of these is Aristotle's distinction between nature *(physis)* and craft *(techne)*. It distinguishes the products of nature from those of human making. The paradigm of natural production is the father who procreates *(gennai),* that of technical production the artisan who makes *(poiei)* *(Met.* VII. 1033b22–23). Three points need to be made here. The first is that Aristotle's distinction is not the same as ours between natural world and humanly created world *(Naturwelt* and *Kulturwelt).* For we tend to take the notion of a product of human making in a wider sense than Aristotle, including under it both his notions of *techne* and of *praxis.* But Aristotle sharply excludes *praxis* from *techne:*

> But making is different from doing (ἕτερον δ'ἐστὶ ποίησις καὶ πρᾶξις). . . . Nor is either of them contained in the other, for doing is not making nor making doing (οὐδὲ περιέχεται ὑπ' ἀλλήλων· οὔτε γὰρ ἡ πρᾶξις ποίησις οὔτε ἡ ποίησις πρᾶξις ἐστί). . . . But as making and doing are distinct, craft must belong to making but not to doing (ἐπεὶ δὲ ποίησις καὶ πρᾶξις ἕτερον, ἀνάγκη τὴν τέχνην ποιήσεως ἀλλ' οὐ πράξεως εἶναι). *(E.N.* VI. 1140a2–17)

This passage is worth quoting in some detail because it positions his theory of art in the Aristotelian rather than in our conceptual space. For Aristotle, unlike us, human activities such as ethical and political life are natural, having their *arche* in human agents and so in human nature, and having their final cause within themselves *(esti gar aute he eupraxia telos; E.N.* VI. 1140b7) because they have no product and hence no final cause beyond themselves *(E.N.* VI. 5,6; cf. *E.N.* I. 1094a3–6; *Met.* IX. 1048b22–23). Understanding the distinctive subject matter of the *Poetics* within the Aristotelian *physis-techne* divide saves one from anachronistically understanding it as a human *praxis.* Instead, it is to be understood as a *techne.*[4]

The second point to be made is that Aristotle's *physis-techne* distinction encompasses being in all categories on either side, since coming to be is either natural or technical in all categories (I here disregard his third distinction, "spontaneously," *tautomatou; Met.* VII. 1032a12–13). *Techne* therefore includes a great variety of rational productive skills in different categories. When its products are in the category of *ousia,* it ranges from the shoemaker's humble craft to the exalted one of a Homer. When they are in the category of quality, it ranges from the physician's honorable craft of bringing his patient back to health to the *rhetor's* questionable one of whipping a mob into a frenzy (though Aristotle vacillates about including the more disreputable aspects of rhetoric in its *techne).* In the category of *ousia, techne* produces new individual *ousiai,* while in the secondary categories it produces new accidental conditions in already existing *ousiai (Met.* VII. 1032a12–15).

Since it is a point of lively contention among Aristotelians whether *techne* can produce *ousiai,* one's understanding of the distinctive subject matter of the *Poetics* requires taking a position in this debate. For what is at stake is the categorial status of a tragedy. If *techne* cannot produce *ousiai*, a tragedy can only be a humanly produced new accidental condition in an already existing natural *ousia*. If *techne* can produce *ousiai*, then the categorial status of a tragedy is being left undecided in this first adumbration of the distinctive subject matter of the *Poetics*. My approach to the *Poetics* includes the position that *techne* can produce *ousiai*, and I again adduce a minimum of supporting argument. The most important of these is that the consequences of a radical denial that *techne* can produce *ousiai* conflict with the overwhelming evidence of many texts and are inherently senseless.

By a radical denial I mean, not a partial one such as Gill's, for whom some artifacts are *ousiai* while others are not; nor a partial one such as Katayama's, for whom artifacts are not *ousiai* only in some senses and by some criteria; but the uncompromising one that what *techne* produces is an *ousia* in any sense, by any criterion, and in any function.[5] Questions of approach benefit, I believe, from clarification in terms of extreme alternatives, which enable us to assess the location of intermediate positions. The radical denial means that the product of a *techne* is neither a composite individual *ousia* nor the constitutive form or matter of one, neither marked by priority in being nor in definition, neither functioning as *pros hen* subject of the inherence of accidental properties nor of accidental predication. All artifacts must then, on pain of falling outside the extension of being and outside Aristotle's distinctive understanding of being altogether, be accidental properties of natural *ousiai*. This means that they must be *pros hen* focused on these *ousiai* and so incapable of being separate from them. An artifact and the natural *ousia* whose accidental property it is, must then form an intercategorial accidental predicative compound such as pale Socrates.

These consequences conflict with the overwhelming evidence of many texts and are inherently senseless. Aristotle treats artifacts on a par with natural *ousiai* as the analysanda of both ontic (i.e., predicative) and ontological (i.e., constitutive) analysis by placing them in the subject position. In ontic analysis he treats them as the *pros hen* subjects of the inherence and so of the predication of accidental properties, potentialities, and changes. In ontological analysis he treats them as *synola*, that is, as entities intracategorially causally constituted by form (actuality) and matter (potentiality) (e.g., *Met.* IX. 7; cf. VIII. 2). They are, however, nonparadigmatic *ousiai*. This enables him to use them as analogues of natural *ousiai*, which he does with remarkable frequency in many texts, for example, "For things different in kind are, we think, completed by different things (we see this to be true both of natural objects and of things produced by craft, e.g., animals, trees, a painting, a sculpture, a house, an implement)" (E.N. X. 1175a22–25; cf. *Phys.* II. 193a31–33).

Analogy is for Aristotle not a vague nontechnical similarity but instead a technical structural one. One thing can be used as an analogue of another only if A:B = C:D, if they are constitutively isomorphic and so illumine one another's inner structure. For Aristotle to use an intercategorial accidental predicative compound (a natural *ousia* in which an artifact inheres as an accidental property) to illumine the inner structure of an *ousia* would be singularly inept, contradictory to his own technical definition of analogy, and wilfully misleading. For it, like pale Socrates, lacks precisely the inner constitutive structure and substantial unity of Socrates, and so it would be used in an analogy in the very respect in which it would not be an analogue. And since neither accidents nor intercategorial accidental predicative compounds can themselves have accidents (*Met.* V. 7; IV. 1007b2–16), artifacts could neither have, nor have predicated of them, any accidental properties, potentialities, or changes. Nor could they be defined in their own right *(haplos)*. Neither could they have any intrinsic meaningfulness or worth. Even for non-Aristotelians, at least some of these consequences would be inherently senseless. If one accepts *techne* as encompassing all categories, the categorial status of a tragedy has not yet been decided, but the possibility that it may be an *ousia* has not been precluded. Certainly Aristotle lists artifacts as *ousiai* (cf. *Met.* XII. 1070a4–7; *E.N.* X. 1175a23–25).

The third point is that Aristotle's *physis-techne* divide only adumbrates but does not yet specify the distinctive subject matter of the *Poetics*, because *techne* at this general level includes both useful and fine art. Indeed, he uses both types of artifacts interchangeably as analogues of natural *ousiai*. A further restriction within the domain of *techne* is needed before we know which precise subject matter the title of the *Poetics* indicates. But whatever is true of all *techne,* will also be true of each of its two main subdivisions, and will indeed be presupposed by each one. It is therefore important to sort out what pertains to *techne* generally and what to artistic *techne* in particular. This way we shall not only know what is true of a tragedy as a product of artistic *techne,* but also understand whether it is true of it *qua* artistic or *qua techne.* This approach corresponds to Aristotle's progression from knowledge of the fact to knowledge of the reasoned fact (from *hoti* to *dioti*), to the clarity with which he always ascertains at which level of generality something pertains to a being. For example, some things are true of Socrates individually, some specifically, some generically, some categorially (cf. *An. Post.* II. 14; I. 24). In order to ascertain what is true of a tragedy *qua techne,* we need to ask what the general relationship between *physis* and *techne* is.

Aristotle leaves no doubt that the relationship between *physis* and *techne* is imitation *(mimesis)*. All *techne* imitates *physis*. He sometimes adds that *techne* can also complete what *physis* cannot finish, but this seems to pertain to *technai* such as medicine, which restores the healthy condition of a natural *ousia*. Since it does this by imitating both a natural state of health and the goal-directed procedures of *physis*, it also falls under the general *mimesis*-characterization of the *techne-physis* relationship (cf. *Phys.* II. 8). The distinctive subject matter of the *Poetics* must then in the first instance be understood in terms of this general notion of *mimesis*, which pertains to it not *qua* artistic but *qua techne*.[6]

Aristotelians are indebted to McKeon for having specified this general notion of *mimesis* and for having carefully distinguished it from its Platonic antecedent:

> Imitation functions . . . as the differentia by which the arts, useful and fine, are distinguished from nature. Art imitates nature, Aristotle was fond of repeating . . . following the same methods as nature would have employed. . . . Imitation, being peculiar to the processes of art, is not found in the processes of nature or of knowledge.[7]

This specification is important because it locates *mimesis* in the processes of *techne* and excludes cognition and the didactic *logoi*, which express our knowledge, from *mimesis*. For Aristotle, a didactic *logos* is *epistemic* and not a *mimesis* because human cognition takes its entire cognitive content from the objects of knowledge, with whose perceptible and intelligible forms it is identical. Cognition is not a *mimesis* but the veridical reception of its objects. *Logos* is excluded from *mimesis*, and *mimesis* will have to be understood in contrast to *logos*. For while the latter is identical with the objects of knowledge in descriptive content, *mimesis* need not be identical with the objects it imitates.[8] *Techne* can imitate the methods and processes of *physis* without its products having the same descriptive content as, and so being copies of, the products of *physis*. This enables Aristotle to understand *techne* as being *mimetic* and yet as producing originals rather than copies. This possibility, I hasten to add, exists only if these products are *ousiai*, for if they are accidental conditions in natural *ousiai* such as health in a patient or belief in a hearer, they are identical in descriptive content with naturally produced health or belief.

It follows, as McKeon has convincingly argued, that the single greatest mistake a modern reader can make is to understand the Aristotelian notion of *mimesis* in the light of, rather than in contrast to, its Platonic forerunner. For consider the distance between them. Aristotelian *techne* imitates the methods and processes of *physis* rather than the descriptive content of the products of *physis*—while Platonic *techne* imitates the descriptive content of the products of *physis*. Therefore, the products of *techne* are not copies of natural things for Aristotle—while they are copies for Plato. A painting of a bed is a *painting* for Aristotle—while it is a *bed* for Plato. Both *physis* and *techne* create originals for Aristotle—while neither one, nor even the demiurge himself, can do so for Plato. For Aristotle, any shoemaker or poet can do what Plato's creator god cannot.

This stunning difference is due to the fact that Aristotle's notion of *mimesis* is much more restricted than, and lacks the pejorative overtones of, that of Plato. It does not condemn the products of *techne* to third-class ontological status as defective copies of defective copies of perfect transcendent originals. It carries no overtones of deceit, illusion, or counterfeit. There is in principle no reason why a painting or a house could not each be a perfect and genuine being in its own right, as what each one is, a good individual of its kind. And successful medical treatment restores genuine health to a patient, not illusory or counterfeit health. Since *mimesis* is focused on the methods and processes of nature, Aristotle's *physis-techne* divide is much more radical than Plato's, allowing for genuine generic and specific differences between the two domains of being, each with genuine generic and specific forms of its own, when *ousiai* are produced. Aristotle is consequently much more respectful of human making, which, he considers, can produce really new things. Understanding the distinctive subject matter of the *Poetics* in terms of Aristotle's general notion of *mimesis* saves one from wrongly seeing it in a Platonic light.

One's understanding is further clarified by emphasizing certain other features of *mimesis*. *Mimesis* relates *physis* and *techne* asymmetrically, since *techne* imitates *physis*, never *physis techne*. *Physis* is, so to say, the senior partner, and its products are the paradigms. Human making orients itself by these paradigms. It does not occur in a vacuum but takes its methodological and procedural bearings from what already is, and indeed from what already is independently of us. *Mimesis* places human making within a cosmic rather than a human cultural context, within a timeless (i.e., everlasting) rather than a historical frame of reference, within objective rather than subjective (individual or societal) guiding norms.

Aristotle discusses *mimesis* most extensively in *Physics* II, though there are scattered remarks in other texts. *Mimesis* means that *physis* and *techne* are similar in terms of the methods and processes by which they bring their respective products into being. These methods and processes are *telic*, not only in the sense that they aim at a result but in the distinctively Aristotelian sense that they aim at a good and in fact at the best possible result. Teleology (*telos* and *to hou heneka* are used interchangeably, e.g., at

Met. V. 1022a6–8; *Phys.* II. 194a27–28) pervades both domains as their most basic common denominator.

It pervades them, not passively as a mere mark at which active natural and technical forces can aim, but as an active causal force, one of Aristotle's four causal *archai,* which in his enumeration he characterizes as "that for the sake of which and the good, for it is the end of all coming to be and change" *(to hou heneka kai t'agathon, telos gar geneseos kai kineseos pases tout' estin); Met.* I. 983a31–32). The equation of that for the sake of which with the good and the end means that *techne's mimesis* of nature's methods and processes is motivated by the striving for the good and therefore is rational, for both Plato and Aristotle would have regarded any human making or doing not so motivated as irrational *(E.N.* I. 1094a1–2). The focus of *mimesis* on nature's methods and processes should therefore not be misread as being merely technological. Nor should the constraint it imposes on human making be underestimated. The good at which both *physis* and *techne* aim cannot be achieved except by these methods and procedures. *"Techne* imitates *physis"* is a completely general statement and has, like many such Aristotelian pronouncements, prescriptive force. It is not merely a statement of fact nor optional for a rational *technites.* Aristotle leaves no doubt as to the complete coincidence of natural and technical methods and processes of production:

> For example, if a house had been a thing made by nature, it would have come into being in the same way as it now does by craft; and if natural things came into being not only by nature but also by craft, they would come into being in the same way as by nature (οἷον εἰ οἰκία τῶν φύσει γιγνομένων ἦν, οὕτως ἂν ἐγίγνετο ὡς νῦν ὑπὸ τῆς τέχνης· εἰ δὲ τὰ φύσει μὴ μόνον φύσει ἀλλὰ καὶ τέχνῃ γίγνοιτο, ὡσαύτως ἂν γίγνοιτο ᾗ πέφυκεν). *(Phys.* II. 199a12–15)

Why should this be so? What is the link between these methods and processes of production and the goodness of the products? The link lies in Aristotle's distinctive understanding of the products' goodness, which is such that being and becoming must be continuous. The good of each thing is not something different from, or over and above, each thing's being, but its own nature as final cause coincides with the formal cause:

> And since nature means two things, the matter and the form, and since the form is the end, and since the others

are for the sake of the end, the form must be the cause which acts as final cause (καὶ ἐπεὶ ἡ φύσις διττή, ἡ μὲν ὡς ὕλη ἡ δ' ὡς μορφή, τέλος δ' αὕτη, τοῦ τέλους δὲ ἕνεκα τἆλλα, αὕτη ἂν εἴη ἡ αἰτία, ἡ οὗ ἕνεκα). (*Phys.* II. 199a30–32)[9]

Final and formal cause are the same in descriptive content, for the good of each thing is simply to be itself as a viable normal individual of its kind. It consists in the immanent constitutive causal functioning of its form and matter, such that the form as determinant actualizes and makes determinate the matter which as potentiality is determinable. Only in this way can a thing actually be, for: "[I]t is not possible for anything indeterminate to be" (*kai apeiroi oudeni estin einai*; *Met.* II. 994b26–27; XI. 1066b1–2; 11–12). *Met.* IX. 7 therefore sanctions *paronymy* as the linguistic form that expresses the status of the constitutive matter as determinable.

For a thing to become good is therefore simply for it to become, to come into actual being. And since that actual being consists in its immanent form-matter (actuality-potentiality) constitution, its coming into being must consist in the coming about of this constitution. The methods of natural as of technical production must consist in the actualizing and determining of matter by form, in the forming of the matter. Being and becoming are directed to the same end and depend on the same causal *archai:* "Again, that for the sake of which and the end belong to the same inquiry as do all those things that are for their sake" (ἔτι τὸ οὗ ἕνεκα καὶ τὸ τέλος τῆς αὐτῆς, καὶ ὅσα τούτων ἕνεκα; *Phys.* II. 194a27–28). And both *physis* and *techne* must follow the same ordered stages in the process of production: "The relation of the later to the earlier stages is therefore the same in the things of nature as in those of *techne*" (ὁμοίως γὰρ ἔχει πρὸς ἄλληλα ἐν τοῖς κατὰ τέχνην καὶ ἐν τοῖς κατὰ φύσιν τὰ ὕστερα πρὸς τὰ πρότερα; *Phys.* II. 199a18–20). Therefore it is absurd *(atopon)* to think that the final cause does not operate in nature just because we do not see her deliberating. In fact, a *techne* does not deliberate either, though a *technites* does (*Phys.* II. 199b26–33).

Aristotle's general notion of *mimesis* might well be called constitutive or structural *mimesis,* because it grounds the constitutive and structural similarity of the things that are and come about by nature and by *techne,* the analogy of *physis* and *techne.* This in turn grounds his extensive use of technically produced things as analogues of naturally produced ones. It is worth emphasizing that *mimesis* at this general level is not in any way representational or *mimetic* in terms of the descriptive content of the specific forms involved. A:B = C:D designates a constitutive or structural similarity in the relationship between form and matter, which holds between natural and technical things irrespective of the descriptive content of their generic and specific natures. It designates the similar functioning of their immanent causally constitutive *archai*. It means that both *physis* and *techne* create under the shared ontologically normative horizon of *ousia*-hood and out of the shared resources of the matter or materials found in the world. Both stand within the commonality of objective cosmic lawfulness, of the norms of constitutive causality, against which neither may offend on pain of producing a being that is not a good individual of its kind. Understanding the distinctive subject matter of the *Poetics* within these general notions of *techne*, of *mimesis*, and of analogy, enables one to isolate its first *mimetic* aspect.

But the above applies only in the category of *ousia*. A house is a technically produced *ousia*, which constitutively or structurally imitates the form-matter constitution of naturally produced *ousiai*, but whose *eidos* has a new descriptive content not found in nature, for nature produces no houses. By contrast, a technically produced accidental condition in an already existing *ousia*, such as health produced in a human being by medical *techne*, constitutively or structurally imitates the *pros hen* dependence of naturally produced health, and therefore its *eidos* does not have a new descriptive content but is identical with that found in nature, for nature produces health in human beings. This difference between *ousia* and the secondary categories of being vividly illustrates the constraints of categorial *pros hen* structure, within which all becoming operates, natural and technical alike. Only being in the category of *ousia* is ontologically and definitorily independent *(choriston)*, and this independence opens up a categorial space for human making of something that is new and independent in descriptive content, in its specific nature or *eidos*. It is precisely this independence that being in the secondary categories lacks, for in its definition that of the *ousia*, whose accidental property it is, must be present (*Met.* VII. 1). The doctor's *techne* lies within more severe natural constraints than the housebuilder's or the poet's, and his *mimesis* allows less scope for innovation.

2.3 *Artistic* Techne *(Mimesis 2)*

But in order to understand the *Poetics* within the notion of artistic *techne* in contrast to non-artistic or useful *(chresimon)*, we must subdivide general *techne* into these two domains. The distinction is based on a second, more restricted notion of *mimesis*, which applies only to artistic *techne*. It is entirely distinct from and presupposes the general notion. All and only the products of artistic *techne* are generically *mimeseis* in this second sense, which is their generic nature and so a genuine subject genus (cf. *An. Post.*

I. 28). It means that all and only works of art have representational content. Aristotle has no notion of nonrepresentational art, and he holds that a useful artifact such as a shoe or a saw has no representational content, and neither of course does the health that successful medical treatment has restored in a patient or the belief or emotion that successful rhetorical speechmaking has produced in an audience.

Aristotle's use of the same word to designate two different *mimetic* aspects in the products of artistic *techne* is justified, because it emphasizes what they have in common. But it is also misleading, since it may obscure how they differ. In order to keep both in view, I propose to designate the more general notion as *mimesis* 1 and the more restricted notion as *mimesis* 2, characterizing the former as constitutive or structural and the latter as representational. While *mimesis* 1 imitates the constitutive functioning of a natural *eidos* in relation to its matter, *mimesis* 2 imitates its descriptive content, such as being a man or an action or an emotion, etc. The analogy of *physis* and *techne* is, however, exclusively based on the former, because analogy is constitutive or structural similarity rather than similarity in descriptive content. Both *mimesis* 1 and *mimesis* 2 are *mimetic* of nature, so that *physis* remains their reference point.

The distinction between the constitutive causal functioning of a thing's *eidos* and its descriptive content (e.g., human nature is biped animal in descriptive content) is explicitly recognized by Aristotle and expressed in two different sorts of metaphysical *logos*, the first functional and the second definitional. A functional *logos* is an account of an *ousia's* intrinsic form-matter (actuality-potentiality) constitution. The most important examples are at *Met.* VII. 17; VIII. 6; IX. 7. A definitional *logos* is an account of the descriptive content of an *ousia's* substantial nature *(eidos)*, listing genus and differentia and is a recurrent theme. At *Met.* IX. 1052b9–15, Aristotle expressly differentiates the descriptive content of elements and causes from their constitutive functioning:

> For in a sense fire is an element . . . but in a sense it is not; for it is not the same thing to be fire and to be an element, but while as a particular thing with a nature of its own fire is an element, the name 'element' means that it has this function, that there is something which is made of it as a primary immanent constituent. And so with cause and one and all others of this sort (ἔστι μὲν γὰρ ὡς στοιχεῖον τὸ πῦρ . . . ἔστι δ᾽ ὡς οὔ· οὐ γὰρ τὸ αὐτὸ πυρὶ καὶ στοιχείῳ εἶναι, ἀλλ᾽ ὡς μὲν πρᾶγμά τι καὶ φύσις τὸ πῦρ στοιχεῖον, τὸ δὲ ὄνομα σημαίνει τὸ τοδὶ συμβεβηκέναι

αὐτῷ ὅτι ἐστί τι ἐκ τούτου ὡς πρώτου ἐνυπάρχοντος.
οὕτω καὶ ἐπὶ αἰτίου καὶ ἑνὸς καὶ τῶν τοιούτων ἁπάντων).

I have translated *symbebekenai* as "function" rather than as "attribute," for the sense of the passage demands it. Aristotle is not distinguishing between fire's own *physis* and an accidental attribute it may have, but rather between that *physis* and its constitutive role in the being of an *ousia*, its functioning as part of the material cause. Given this differentiation, it is not surprising that a different kind of *mimesis* pertains to an artifact's constitution and to its descriptive content.

Mimesis 2 as the generic nature of all products of artistic *techne* means that the distinctive subject matter of the *Poetics* must be approached definitionally within this notion, since the generic nature is part of a thing's definition. It is common to verbal, partly verbal, and nonverbal species of art alike. Aristotle makes no generic distinction between verbal and nonverbal art, according them a deeper commonality than we might be inclined to do. At the same time, their shared generic nature is just having representational content, nothing further. It is not beauty, so that titles such as *The Arts of the Beautiful* are not Aristotelian, however fine this particular book's understanding of Aristotle's nondidactic ontology of art may be.[10] An aesthetizing approach to the *Poetics* would be misleading. Beauty is not part of Aristotle's definition of a tragedy, and his paradigm of beauty is a living organism rather than a work of art (cf. *De Partibus Animalium* I.5).

2.4 Poetical Techne, Tragic Techne

Approaching the distinctive subject matter of the *Poetics* by way of general and artistic *techne* enables us to understand its title, *Aristotle's About Poetical Techne*. It narrows *techne* down from its general to its generic to its subgeneric level of poetical art. But it does not narrow it down to its specific level of tragic art. The treatise's dealing with artistic *techne* generically as well as subgenerically and specifically is in accord with Aristotle's normal approach to any subject matter. For to understand anything in its specific nature is for him inseparable from placing it within its generic and subgeneric context. The title is subgeneric, because the *Poetics* was meant to deal with both tragedy and comedy. We know from Diotima in Plato's *Symposium* that *poiesis* (and hence *poietike*) was used at different levels of generality (205 b–d).

The distinctive subject matter of the *Poetics* is linked with its location in the *corpus,* as can be seen in the following schema:

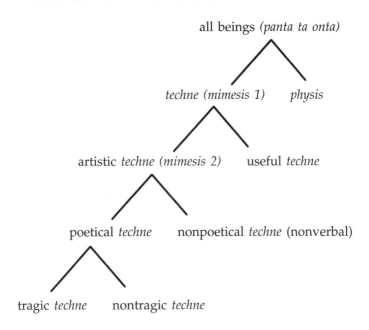

all beings *(panta ta onta)*

techne (mimesis 1)   *physis*

artistic *techne (mimesis 2)*   useful *techne*

poetical *techne*   nonpoetical *techne* (nonverbal)

tragic *techne*   nontragic *techne*

It is delineated by keeping to the left side of the descent from the unrestricted extension of being. And one understands a tragedy in terms of what pertains to it at each level of this descent: *qua* being, *qua* a product of *techne*, *qua* a product of artistic *techne*, *qua* a product of poetical *techne*, *qua* a product of tragic *techne*. Its location in the *corpus* is determined by its relationships with the other texts that elucidate what each *qua* means.

2.5 Tragedy as an Ousia

One final question needs to be answered before this description of the approach to the *Poetics'* subject matter and location in the *corpus* is complete. That is the question of the categorial status of a tragedy. Is a tragedy an *ousia* or a technically produced new accidental condition in an already existing *ousia*? Is it an analogue of a human being or of the health that medical *techne* has produced in a human being? Is it ontologically separate *(choriston)* or *pros hen* dependent on another *ousia*?

This question cannot be avoided unless one argues that a tragedy falls outside the extension of being or outside Aristotle's distinctive understanding of being, and that therefore the *Poetics* cannot be approached in terms of the above schema. No such argument has been given, and there is no textual evidence for it either in the *Poetics* or outside it. As will be argued in chapter 3, the *Poetics* shows Aristotle's use of his distinctive understanding of being. To the best of my knowledge, the categorial question has not been posed explicitly as a metatheoretic reflection about one's approach to the *Poetics*, though the ontological status of artifacts has been discussed in relation to other texts. This omission has been unfortunate, because it has led to wrong principles and criteria for the establishment, translation, and exegesis of the text, to misreception.

It is clear that a great deal hinges on one's categorial approach, not only because the distinction between *ousia* and the secondary categories of being is pervasive and fundamental in Aristotle's thought, but because in categorizing a tragedy one commits oneself to all that this entails. Categorial status determines a being's inner structure, its definability, its ability to function as ontic and predicative subject, and whether it can be self-referential, self-significant, and self-worthy.[11] The full significance of categorization is often obscured by translations that still render *einai* as "exist" rather than as "be," where "be" carries the "fused" sense explained by Furth.[12] The *pros hen* dependence of being in the secondary categories on *ousia* is "fused," not merely existential, so that it is literally adjectival *(paronymous)*. Some of its implications for *techne* have already been developed in Section 2.2 above.

Can the above schema help us to find an answer? I believe so, but beyond that it can help to clarify the question by pinpointing at which level the reason for the answer lies. The schema's first level, *panta ta onta,* leaves both possibilities open, for *qua* being, a tragedy could be either an *ousia* or an accident of an already existing *ousia*. *Qua* being, however, it must be one or the other. Aristotle recognizes both natural and man-made *ousiai*, e.g., "[E]ach *ousia* comes into being out of something that shares its name (this is true of natural and of the other *ousiai*)" (*Met.* XII. 1070a4–6).

The second level, *techne (mimesis* 1) also seems to leave both possibilities open, for *qua* product of *techne* a tragedy could be either an *ousia* or an accident of an already existing *ousia,* since *techne* can produce either. But *qua* product of *techne,* we can now specify what being an *ousia* and what being an accident of an already existing *ousia* entails for a tragedy, and that specification gives us an answer. As argued above, being a technically produced *ousia* means that a tragedy constitutively or structurally imitates the form-matter constitution of a naturally produced *ousia,* while its *eidos* has a new descriptive content not found in nature, for nature produces no tragedies. By contrast, being an accident of an already existing *ousia* means that a tragedy would constitutively or structurally imitate the *pros hen* dependence of a naturally produced accident on an *ousia,* and therefore its *eidos* would not have new descriptive content but be identical with that found in nature. Nature would then produce tragedies as accidents of already existing *ousiai,* just as it produces health in human beings. For the constraints of categorial *pros hen* structure do not allow something new and independent to come into being in any secondary category, since in the *logos* of accidental being that of the *ousia* whose accident it is must be present. If nature cannot produce a tragedy as an accident of an already existing *ousia*, neither can *techne*, just as, if nature could not produce health in a human being, a doctor could not either. Only *ousia* opens up a categorial space for human making of something that is new and independent in descriptive content, in its specific nature *(eidos)*. If the tragic *(to tragikon)* is art-specific for Aristotle (i.e., not found in nature or in human life), then a tragedy whose *eidos* it is, must be an *ousia*.

The tragic *(to tragikon)* is indeed art-specific for Aristotle, as in classical Greek generally. Greek usage is here fundamentally different from English, and the latter is severely misleading in approaching the *Poetics*. In English we call both a tragedy and a human life tragic, in fact, we call a great many other things tragic as well. These range from an entire historical epoch to single actions to misunderstandings to coincidences. The term is not art-specific and is transferred from life to the stage, so that we might see a tragedy as the imitation of a tragic action rather than as the tragic imitation *(tragike mimesis)* of an action. The placement of "tragic" in the last clause spells the difference between us and Aristotle. For him, the tragic is a specific nature in the generic nature *mimesis* 2, it is art-specific and transferred from the stage to life only in ironical and pejorative uses such as "in the tragic manner" or "bombastic" *(tragikos)*. In Anton's memorable formulation:

> For Aristotle, the political man, the statesman, is not a
> tragic artist, nor is life itself tragic. The "tragic sense" of
> life is a modern, indeed a neo-Christian invention, with
> Nietzsche being its chief prophet and preacher.[13]

As art-specific, the tragic is only a product of *techne*, not of *physis*, and therefore new and independent in descriptive content. This gives it the categorial status of an *ousia*. The question how the new and independent descriptive content of its specific nature *(eidos)* can be reconciled with its *mimetic* 2 generic nature *(genos)*, will find its full answer in chapters 3 and 4. Two points concerning it have, however, already been made. In Section 2.2 above, McKeon's differentiation between Plato's and Aristotle's notions of *mimesis* has yielded the point that while a painting of a bed is a *bed* for Plato, it is a *painting* for Aristotle. The juxtaposition of our modern characterization of a tragedy as the imitation of a tragic action with Aristotle's as the tragic imitation of an action *(tragike mimesis)* has yielded the point that the tragic nature of this *mimesis* 2 is not a copy but an original. The two points converge: a tragedy is a new substantial being.

A few further arguments can be adduced here. First, the categorial status of a tragedy must be consistent through the entire left-hand descent from *panta ta onta*. It could not be an *ousia qua* being or *qua* product of *techne*, but an accident of an already existing *ousia qua* product of artistic or tragic *techne*. Second, the more general levels are presupposed by, prior to, and authoritative for, the less general ones. This is a general feature of Aristotle's approach to any subject matter, where the less general specifies, but does not contradict, the more general. *Mimesis* 1 is prior to *mimesis* 2, and since the former gives a tragedy the categorial status of an *ousia*, the latter must incorporate representational content into that status. Third, there is simply no already existing *ousia* available, whose *pros hen* dependent accident a tragedy could be.

Only two *ousiai* could be considered for this role, both individual human beings. One is the playwright as the efficient cause who makes it, the other is the recipient as the patient who reads or sees it performed. Only a concrete individual *ousia* can serve as ontic and predicative subject of *pros hen* dependent accidents, and such a subject is *paronymously* characterized by its accidents. The playwright cannot serve as ontic and predicative subject for a tragedy because this would reduce *techne* or *poiesis* to *praxis* and be incompatible with his role as efficient cause of the tragedy. Aristotle very carefully distinguishes *techne* or *poiesis* from *praxis* and the process of making from its product at *Met.* IX.1050a23–33:

> But since in some cases the activity is the end (for example, seeing that of sight, and nothing different comes to be from sight beyond the seeing), while from some activities something comes to be (for example, from the craft of building a house beyond the activity of building), so in the former case the end of the potentiality is in the activity itself, while in the latter case it is rather in the thing made. For the activity of building is realized in the thing that is built, and it comes to be and is at the same time as the house. Where, then, what comes to be is something different and beyond *(heteron kai para)* the activity, there the actuality is in the thing produced; for example, the activity of building is actualized in the thing built and the activity of weaving in the thing that is woven, and similarly in all other cases . . .[14]

This long quote is by no means an isolated statement. A house cannot be an accidental attribute of the builder, a patient's health cannot be an attribute of the doctor, and a tragedy cannot be an attribute of the playwright. The builder, the doctor, and the playwright are efficient causes of their respective products, while the human being who sees is the *ousia* of his seeing, which is his activity and hence his accidental attribute. Efficient causality and the relation of an *ousia* to its own activities are entirely distinct for Aristotle, and the former is incompatible with *paronymous* characterization in terms of the product. The builder cannot be said to be housey (or some such locution), the doctor cannot be said to be healthy with the patient's health, and the playwright cannot be said to be tragic, while the human being who sees can and must be said to be seeing (cf. *Met.* VII. 1; IX. 7). "Being a *pros hen* accident of the playwright" and "having been produced by the playwright" are not only different but mutually exclusive, for an *ousia* does not produce its accidental attributes by efficient causality. Otherwise every *praxis* would be a *poiesis* or *techne*. The product's ontological independence *(para)* from its producer is one of the most welcome features of Aristotle's careful distinction between efficient causality and the *ousia*-accident relation, between *techne* and *praxis*. But ontological independence means that the product cannot be *pros hen* dependent on its producer. It is therefore definable independently of him and can be self-referential, self-significant, and self-worthy.[15]

Nor, for some of the same reasons, could a tragedy be a *pros hen* dependent attribute of an individual human being, who reads or sees it performed, a recipient or patient. *Pros hen* dependence is always of an individual being in a secondary category on an individual *ousia* and means that the accident is incapable of being separate *(choriston)* from the *ousia*, that it is an aspect of the *ousia's* own being, and that the *ousia* is *paronymously* characterized in terms of it. An individual house or a tragedy can be separate from an individual owner or recipient, unlike an individual state of health, which cannot be separate from the patient whose health it is. The modern attempt to liken a tragedy to a patient's health in categorial status, conceptualizing it as something potential when not actively received, is not Aristotelian. A potential and an actualized accident are both *pros hen* dependent on the same *ousia*. For Aristotle recognizes no unattached accidents, neither potential nor actual ones. The patient's health, when not actually present in him, does not exist potentially separate from him, but rather *pros hen* dependent on him as an accidental potentiality that he has.[16] His health, whether actual or potential, is an aspect of his own human being, since it is human health that has human nature present in its definition.

Neither a house nor a tragedy is either a potential or an actual aspect of a human being, since neither has human nature present in its definition. And while a patient is *paronymously* said to be either potentially or actually healthy, a human being cannot be said to be either potentially or actually housey or tragic. The house and the tragedy are ontologically independent *(choriston)* from an owner and from a recipient, surely a welcome feature of Aristotle's fundamental distinction between *ousia* and the secondary categories of being, which is prior to his distinction between potentiality and actuality. The products of *techne* that have the categorial status of an *ousia* emancipate themselves both from their makers and from their recipients. As a result they are definable in their own being *(haplos)* independently of either, and they can be self-referential, self-significant, and self-worthy.

Determining a tragedy's categorial status as an *ousia* completes my approach to the distinctive subject matter of the *Poetics* and to its location in the *corpus*. In terms of the above schema, a tragedy is a being in the category of *ousia*, a product of *techne* (*mimesis* 1), of artistic *techne* (*mimesis* 2), of poetical *techne*, of tragic *techne*. All that is entailed by each level pertains to its being. It is this entire sequence that yields principles and criteria for the reception of the *Poetics*. Key among them is *ousia*. For if a tragedy is an *ousia*, the *Poetics* has to be read principally in the light of the *Metaphysics* and only secondarily in the light of the *Rhetoric* and of the *Nicomachean Ethics* (with the *Politics* in the background of either). The *Metaphysics* lays out the constitutive structure, *archai*, and criteria of substantial being and so provides the template in terms of which a tragedy's essential being must be understood. Since *ousia* is prior to all secondary categories, the *Metaphysics* is prior in importance to the *Rhetoric* and to the *Nichomachean Ethics*, which do not bear on a tragedy's essential being. Their bearing on the *Poetics* will be discussed in chapter 4. A tragedy is to be understood in contrast to them. I need not and do not deny the relevance of the two latter texts. But I do deny that they are either prior to or equal in importance to the former. In this point the approach of the present study differs from that of most others.[17]

Chapter 3

LEVELS WITHIN THE *POETICS*

My approach to the *Poetics* has been a gradual narrowing down from the *corpus* as a whole to its own subject matter and location. This, I believe, accords with Aristotle's normal procedure. But the narrowing down must not be understood merely quantitatively. Each level of generality contains features that pertain to the being of a tragedy. That being can be understood fully and clearly only when each feature is traced to its proper level. I now recapitulate these levels briefly.

The most general level is that of being, the unrestricted extension of being *(panta ta onta)*, which comprises whatever is. Aristotle conceptualizes it as being, so that his entire *corpus* is philosophy of being, whose systematic or doctrinal content consists of the following pervasive substantive-methodological conceptual constants: the concept of being, the categories of being, the categorial priority of *ousia,* immanent causal form-matter constitution in the category of *ousia,* and the ontological and cognitive priority of the object. These constitute his distinctive understanding of being.

The next general level is that of craft *(techne),* which comprises all products of human making in all categories *(poiesis* in the most general sense) and relates them to the products of nature *(physis)* in terms of structural or constitutive imitation *(mimesis* 1). The next is that of artistic craft or art, which comprises all products of human artistic making in the category of *ousia (poiesis* in a narrower sense) and relates them to the

35

products of nature in terms of representational imitation (*mimesis* 2). Next is poetical art which comprises all products of verbal art (the *poietikes technes* of the title of the *Poetics*), and finally tragic poetry which comprises all products of the tragic playwright's art (*tragike mimesis; Poetics* 26.1461b26). The full understanding of a tragedy is therefore as follows: it is a being, it is a product of human craft, it is a product of artistic craft or art, it is a product of verbal art or poetry, it is a product of tragic poetry. Each level below the most general (*panta ta onta*) conceptualizes a tragedy as a product of human making, and each specifies it more and more precisely, until it reaches the tragic (*to tragikon*) as the specific nature (the *eidos*) of this product.

Chapters 1 and 2 have presented this approach, based on explicit evidence in texts other than the *Poetics*. Chapter 3 will test it against the *Poetics* itself. Some of the above levels are explicitly present in it, some only implicitly. Chapter 3 will therefore use two kinds of textual evidence, direct and indirect. Direct evidence is explicit statement, indirect evidence is of two kinds, namely, absence of any indication that the features that pertain to a level are not relevant, and use of these features.

3.1 The First Level: Being

The features pertaining to this level are not explicitly present in the *Poetics*, which contains no statements to the effect that a tragedy is one of the things that are and that it is to be conceptualized in terms of Aristotle's distinctive understanding of being. That is not surprising, since this short text has a definite subject matter of its own. The textual evidence for the implicit presence of the features of the first level is therefore indirect, consisting both of the absence of any textual indication that they are not relevant and of indications of their use.

The absence of any textual indication is an argument from silence, never conclusive in itself but carrying some weight in conjunction with other evidence. For there is a reasonable *prima facie* presumption that Aristotle's distinctive understanding of being, as delineated in completely general statements, applies to any individual treatise, especially one that shows indications of the use of its features. Anyone arguing that it does not would need to point to some textual support. What would count as such support? Something that would, in Owen's phrase, "make any reader of the *Metaphysics* or of the *Nicomachean Ethics* rub his eyes."[1] He found something like this in *E.E.* I. 8, where Aristotle fell into *aporia* concerning the possibility of a general *episteme* of the good or of being, an *aporia* he resolved in terms of his distinctive understanding of being in the *Metaphysics* and the *Nicomachean Ethics*. Since the presence of that very understanding in the *Poetics* is now at issue, the textual support needed to argue against it would have to be similar to what Owen found in *E.E.* I. 8. It might be the statement of an *aporia*, which he elsewhere resolves in terms of his distinctive understanding of being; it might be an expression of doubt or hesitation concerning the applicability of his normal first principles and so of his ability to conceptualize and comprehend (let alone define!) a tragedy; it might be a casting about for a method of approach; it might also be the statement or use of some alternative conceptualization, such as one that gives priority to becoming over being or one that understands a tragedy not in terms of the fixity of being but of the flux of historical development or of the unpredictable creative originality of playwrights.

What we find in the *Poetics* is the precise opposite of all these. There is nothing in the text that would make any reader of the *Metaphysics* or the *Nicomachean Ethics* rub his eyes. Halliwell notes:

> The greatest problem facing many readers of the *Poetics* today is an inevitable lack of sympathy with the spirit of Ar.'s enterprise. The work's very first sentence is likely to reveal the problem at once, by the characteristic confidence which it shows in the rational, methodical and objective character of the philosopher's quest for a comprehension of poetry and its values. . . . The rational confidence exhibited and embodied in the *Poetics*—which we see immediately in the prescriptive note struck at the start, and in the invocation of "first principles."[2]

This confidence never wavers. It enables Aristotle not only to characterize a tragedy but to give a formal definition of it—surely the height of rational confidence. It makes him critical of even the greatest tragic playwrights, of audiences, of actors, and of stagecraft. Far from formulating *aporiai* himself, he resolves those formulated by others. And, as commentators have noted, it leads him to take considerable liberties with the empirical material, the tragedies themselves.[3] His rational confidence is rooted in his own philosophy, in his own first principles, rather than in the authority of any playwright, of any other philosopher, or of the prestige of any tragedy. There is no textual indication that these first principles are anything other than those involved in his own distinctive understanding of being. The mood and tone of the treatise, coupled with indications of the use of the features of that understanding, make the argument from silence uncommonly strong.

Textual indications of the use and foundational importance of these features abound, and the following is but a selective presentation:

3.1.1 The Concept of Being

The clearest textual indication that Aristotle conceptualizes a tragedy in terms of being is found in chapters 4 and 5 of the *Poetics,* which in sketching its developmental history, firmly subordinate it to the fixity of being. He traces the causes of poetry's coming into being *(gennesai)* to factors in human nature *(aitiai physikai,* which are *symphyton tois anthropois;* 4.1448b4–22), and he traces the causes of its successive stages of development to the nature and special gifts of poets *(kata ta oikeia ethe, kata ten oikeian physin,* with Homer as the *malista poietes;* 4.1448b22–9a6). These are efficient causes of the becoming of poetry, which operate within the constraints of the final causality exerted by a tragedy's own nature, its own essential being. Becoming, in the *Poetics* as everywhere else in Aristotle, lies within the bounds of definite being *(ek tinos eis ti).* Final causality, here as everywhere else, is superior to efficient causality in explanatory power. It guides the process of development toward what a tragedy is, so that its becoming must ultimately be understood in terms of its being. And when it has reached that immanent *telos,* it stops further becoming:

> And having gone through many changes, tragedy stopped itself, since it had attained its own nature (καὶ πολλὰς μεταβολὰς μεταβαλοῦσα ἡ τραγῳδία ἐπαύσατο, ἐπεὶ ἔσχε τὴν αὐτῆς φύσιν). (4.1449a14–15)

This striking sentence is almost impossible to express in English, largely because its impersonal language focuses on the objective being and active final causality of a tragedy in a way that minimizes the efficient causality of the human agents. It also focuses on the fixity of a tragedy's own being, which cuts off further development because it would violate the nature already attained and so produce tragedies that would not be good individuals of their kind. The final cause lies in the product of any human making and coincides with the product's own formal cause or nature. Impersonal language dominates the entire *Poetics,* and the ascription of a nature *(physis)* to a product of human making recurs here as elsewhere. Commentators seem to be in agreement that final causality is paramount: "[T]he tragic form, like an organic growth, develops until it reaches its *telos,* when its potentiality is fully realized."[4] They perhaps do not adequately stress how completely this text is in accord with Aristotle's general philosophy of being and how matter-of-factly he subsumes artistic *techne* under it.

3.1.2 The Categories of Being

There is no explicit list or statement of the categories of being in the *Poetics* nor an explicit statement that a tragedy is to be understood in their light. But they are used, both individually and in contrast to each other. The most important individual use is that of the category of *ousia* in chapter 6, where Aristotle proposes to give a formal definition of tragedy (*horon tes ousias*; 6.1449b23–24). The very formality with which he introduces it, the explicit backward reference to the already delineated genus-species-differentiae parameters of definition in chapters 1–3,[5] and his repeated contrast between what a tragedy is in itself and in relation to the audience (e.g., *auto te kath hauto . . . kai pros ta theatra*; 4.1449a8–9) make it all but certain that *ousia* here carries its normal categorial sense. The contrast between the categories of *ousia* and *pros ti* is the most important for Aristotle, and it recurs in the contrast between what pertains to tragic poetry essentially and what pertains to it accidentally (*kath hauten . . . kata symbebekos*; chapter 25, which bases its solution of *aporiai* formulated by others on this contrast). The familiar categorial distinction of essence and accident is used not only in this context but also in his discussion of the proper length of a tragedy, which is in the secondary category of quantity (*tou de mekous horos* or *megethos*, chapter 7) and in his contrast between the constitutive parts of a tragedy (which determine its qualitative nature) and its quantitative parts (*poia tis*; 6.1450a8 and *kata to poson*; 12.1452b15). The categories of being are implicitly present.

3.1.3 The Categorial Priority of Ousia

The priority of *ousia* is not explicitly asserted in the *Poetics*, but both its use and the contrasts between it and other categories imply it. For its use is definitory, and the contrasts deny definitory significance to other categories, particularly to *pros ti*.

The use of *ousia* in the formal definition of tragedy at the beginning of chapter 6 has already been alluded to, and some reasons for believing that *ousia* here carries its normal categorial meaning have been given. These will now be amplified. If this definition is indeed in the category of *ousia* (i.e., if the *ousia* or essence to be defined is that of an entity that is an *ousia* rather than an accident of some other *ousia*), and if it enjoys the kind of priority that such definition has in Aristotle's distinctive understanding of being, then it should conform to his distinctive concept of substantial definition. It should reflect the definitional priority of *ousia* by being stated in an unqualified manner (*haplos*), i.e., all its definitory parts should be intracategorially contained in the category of *ousia*, so that none should fall into any secondary category. It should not contain the definition of any other *ousia,* nor should it be said to be the definition of a quality, a quantity, or a relation (such as *horos tou megethous* at 7.1451a15). The definition of tragedy meets this test. Its introduction explicitly refers back to what has already been said and quite emphatically states that the definition arises out of it (περὶ δὲ τραγῳδίας λέγωμεν ἀναλαβόντες αὐτῆς ἐκ τῶν εἰρημένων τὸν γινόμενον ὅρον τῆς οὐσίας; 6.1449b22–24). The definition arises out of, and so can be expected to be in conformity with, the genus-species-differentiae account with which the *Poetics* begins and which is elaborated in chapters 1—3. The expectation of conformity engendered by this introduction is the stronger as the sentence containing the definition follows immediately upon it. But the genus-species-differentiae parameters of definition spelled out in the second sentence of the *Poetics* contain nothing that straddles different categories; instead they are stated *haplos:* "Now, epic and tragic poetry as well as comedy and dithyramb (and most of music for the pipe or lyre) are, taken all together, kinds of imitation. But they are differentiated from one another by three things: namely, by imitating through different materials, or different objects, or in different manners rather than in the same manner" (1.1447a13–18). The generic nature, *mimesis,* is differentiated into specific natures by means of three types of differentiae, which are responsive to the generic nature itself. They are modes of imitating, modes of having representational content. They contain no reference to any secondary category nor to any other *ousia.* What is more, Aristotle in his subsequent elaboration adds no other types of differentiae nor modifies the original three. Their causally constitutive role as differentiating the generic nature into specific natures is emphasized in the recurrent causal language of chapters 1–3, and this marks them as first principles in Aristotle's distinctive understanding of being.[6]

   In the first sentence of the text Aristotle announces that he will begin with first principles *(apo ton proton).* In the second sentence he identifies the three types of differentiae that are the first principles. In the last sentence of chapter 3 (which ends this section of the work) he states that both their number and their nature have now been delineated: "Concerning the differentiae of imitation, both how many and of what kind they are, let these remarks suffice" (3.1448b2–3). In characteristic fashion, he gives their list authoritatively as final and complete with regard to both their number and their nature, and the imperative force of "let these remarks suffice" *(eirestho tauta)* does not leave open the possibility of there being either more types of differentiae or of these three types being understood differently. If he had wanted to indicate that the list was incomplete or that the nature of these differentiae had not yet been adequately understood, he could quite easily have done so.

It is the section of the text ended by this last sentence, to which the introduction of the formal definition of tragedy in chapter 6 explicitly refers back and out of which the definition arises. What separates them are the two chapters that sketch the historical development, but these are in accord with the fixity of being indicated by his authoritative delineation of the number and nature of the differentiae. For it is the nature of tragedy *(ten hautes physin)* that, acting as impersonal final cause, stops further development. And the nature of a thing is precisely the generic nature differentiated into a specific nature by the differentiae. The definitional accounts of the being of a tragedy in chapters 1–3 and 6 are then continuous, and the last sentence of chapter 3 creates a strong expectation that the formal definition will be given in terms of the three types of differentiae, which are all intracategorial, i.e., they are all in the category of *ousia*.

This expectation is confirmed by Aristotle's explicitly subsuming the six constitutive parts *(mere)* of a tragedy under these three types of differentiae in chapter 6:

> Every tragedy must have six parts which make it what it is. These are *mythos, ethe, lexis, dianoia, opsis, melopoiia*. For the materials by means of which tragedies imitate are two of these parts, the manner in which they imitate is one, the objects which they imitate are three. And beyond these there is nothing. (6.1450a7–12)

The subsumption of the six constitutive parts under these three types of differentiae closes with an even more authoritative assertion of their finality and completeness than the end of chapter 3: "And beyond these there is nothing" *(kai para tauta ouden)*. If one takes chapters 4 and 5 as an excursus into historical development, which interrupts the definitional genus-species-differentiae account of a tragedy, then the formal definition itself is framed by two authoritative assertions of the completeness of this account, which are no more than thirty Bekker lines distant from each other and are explicitly tied together in the text both by the introduction of the definition and by the subsumption of the six constitutive parts under the differentiae. At 6.1450a12 the definitional account is complete. What follows is elaboration and a functional account. (For the difference between a definitional and a functional account, see Section 2.3 above).

The formal definition and the spelling out of the meaning of the terms used in it, which are framed in this way in such close textual proximity, could not reasonably contain anything that contradicts this framing without raising serious questions either about Aristotle himself or about the status of the text. Aristotle himself is probably the clearest and most systematic thinker of Greek antiquity, and the text is well established.[7] Moreover, his spelling out of the meaning of the terms used in the definition, "I mean" (lego; 6.1449b28), consists in a typical Aristotelian analysis of the definition into constitutive parts (mere). These are normally the generic nature and the differentiae, and their designation as parts (mere or moria) raises the central metaphysical problem of how such parts can combine to form a real substantial unity. He solves this general problem in Met. VIII. 6. The six constitutive parts are, as intracategorial, in the category of ousia; so too are the three types of differentiae. This enables Aristotle to subsume them under the differentiae. They are implied by the terms used in the definition and spell out the descriptive content of the differentiae. The framing of the definition, its wording, the spelling out of the meaning of that wording, the analysis in terms of constitutive parts and in terms of differentiae are continuous with each other. At no point is this definitional account intercategorial, and it is stated in an unqualified manner (haplos). At no point is it said to be the definitional account of an accident.

Turning now to the definition itself, we find that its connection with its immediately preceding introduction is strengthened by a backward reference which carries some consequential import, oun, translated as "then" by Halliwell. "Tragedy" is the subject of the entire sentence, which contains only one main verb, "is" (esti). The essential being (ti esti) of a tragedy is here defined haplos, in completely objective and impersonal language, and all grammatical references lead back to tragodia:

> Tragedy, then, is an imitation of an action which is serious, complete, and has some magnitude, by means of language which is garnished in various forms in its different parts, by means of dramatic enactment and not narrative, achieving the clarification of how pitiful and ⌣ fearsome actions cause like things to befall (ἔστιν οὖν τραγῳδία μίμησις πράξεως σπουδαίας καὶ τελείας μέγεθος ἐχούσης, ἡδυσμένῳ λόγῳ χωρὶς ἑκάστῳ τῶν εἰδῶν ἐν τοῖς μορίοις, δρώντων καὶ οὐ δι' ἀπαγγελίας, δι' ἐλέου καὶ φόβου περαίνουσα τὴν τῶν τοιούτων παθημάτων κάθαρσιν). (6.1449b24–28)[8]

A tragedy is generically a mimesis 2, differentiated into a specific nature, a tragike mimesis, by the three types of differentiae: the object of imitation (praxeos), the material of imitation (logoi), the manner of imitation (di' dronton). By language (logoi) he means language with rhythm (rhythmon) and melody (harmonian, melos), lyric poetry (melopoiia) and the composition of spoken meters *(lexis)*. Dramatic enactment *(di' dronton)* implies visual spectacle *(opseos kosmos)*. Action *(praxeos)* implies plot-structure *(mythos)*, characters *(ethe)*, articulated rationality *(dianoia)* (6.1449b28–50a7). This elucidation of the meaning of the formal definition is summed up in a most authoritative way as the six constitutive parts: "Hence every tragedy must have six parts" *(ananke oun pases tes tragodias mere einai hex;* 6.1450a7–8). The "must" in connection with "hence" and "every" leaves no doubt that the six parts spell out the meaning of the definition and are the descriptive content of the differentiae. They constitute what a tragedy is *(kath ho poia tis estin he tragodia;* 6.1450a8–9). They are plot-structure *(mythos)*, characters *(ethe)*, language *(lexis)*, articulated rationality *(dianoia)*, spectacle *(opsis)*, lyric poetry *(melopoiia)*. Three of them are subsumed under objects of imitation *(mythos, ethe, dianoia)*, two under materials of imitation *(lexis, melopoiia)*, one under manner of imitation *(opsis)* (6.1450a10–11).[9] The definition now has its completed descriptive content.

The great puzzle for Aristotle's commentators, though apparently not for Aristotle himself, is why "achieving the *katharsis*" is not elucidated. The reason is that it is not a constitutive part in its own right, let alone an additional type of differentia. But if it is not such a part or differentia in its own right, then it must fall under one of the six parts and so under one of the three differentiae. And indeed it does. It falls under the action *(praxeos)* and so under the differentia objects of imitation *(ha)* (see *Poetics* 6.1450a11). The *katharsis,* which a tragedy must achieve (or perhaps complete), relates to the action. It follows that the action is characterized twice in the definition, at the start as serious, complete, and having some magnitude, and at the end as having an achieved or completed *katharsis.* The action is singled out. An imitation is tragic only insofar as the action meets both characterizations, and the one placed at the end is designated as the one which the tragedy must achieve (or complete).

The language is objective and impersonal. The present active participle "achieving" *(perainousa)* has "tragedy" for its subject and is linked with "is" *(esti)* as the only main verb. The tragedy itself must achieve something that is of definitional importance for it, without which it cannot be a tragic imitation. It is in its own essential nature a tragic imitation by achieving this *katharsis,* which in the wording of the definition appears as its direct accusative object. Such impersonal language (however odd to us) is characteristic of Aristotle and designates formal-final causality as it operates in the being of things. Things themselves strive to become and to be what they are, and they may succeed in achieving this to a greater or lesser extent and so be better or worse individuals of their kind. What a tragedy must achieve is its own *ousia,* its own essential being, and central to that is the achievement of the *katharsis* of the action.

It will be a better or worse individual of its kind most crucially in terms of this achievement, and this marks the clarified action as immanent final cause or *telos*. Linking the subject, the main verb, the participle, and the participle's direct accusative object, one gets: *estin tragodia mimesis perainousa ten katharsin.*

The *katharsis* to be achieved is the clarification of the action's sequential-causal structure *(dia).* The meaning of "action" *(praxeos)* as used in the definition is elucidated by Aristotle as *mythos:* "But the imitation of the action is the *mythos*, for by this *mythos* I mean the structure of the action" (ἔστιν δὲ τῆς μὲν πράξεως ὁ μῦθος ἡ μίμησις, λέγω γὰρ μῦθον τοῦτον τὴν σύνθεσιν τῶν πραγμάτων; 6.1450a3–5). It is *mythos* in this technical and innovative sense of structure *(synthesis* or *systasis*, perceptively translated as "plot-structure" by Halliwell)[10] that specifies the meaning of the term used in the definition as one of the six constitutive parts. The selective emphasis on its structure comports well with the selective emphasis on the *katharsis* of this structure in the definition itself. It is characterized as causal *(dia)* both in the definition and in its subsequent elaboration in the next seven chapters (e.g., *tade dia tade;* 10.1452a21). Aristotle's selective emphasis on it is so great that even as sympathetic a commentator as Halliwell finds it "extreme."[11] Aristotle, we may presume, did not find it so. What he meant by *katharsis* is spelled out in two ways: the sequential-causal structure of the complex action must be perspicacious and rationally comprehensible as being by necessity or probability *(ex anankes e kata to eikos* or *hos epi to poly*—used in the text in either version); it must not allow the intrusion of anything that could disrupt or obscure it, such as anything irrational *(alogon),* anything fortuitous *(hopothen etychen, hopou etyche),* any reference to the preferences of actors *(agonismata)* or of audiences *(euchen tois theatais),* any *deus ex machina (apo mechanes),* any contrivance or subjective preference of the poet *(ha bouletai ho poietes all' ouch ho mythos).*

But this causal-structural clarity is only one aspect of the complex action, even though it is the one most emphasized by Aristotle. The action also has objective emotive content. It is pitiful and fearsome.[12] For the actions that compose it are afflictions *(pathemata),* their impact on the protagonists is destructive and painful, involving the radical and unforeseen (or even unforeseeable, *para doxan)* change in fortune. What the tragedy must achieve is the clarification of how pitiful and fearsome actions cause such things to befall *(ten katharsin ton toiouton pathematon di' eleou kai phobou;* [with some change in word-order]). Emotive content is incorporated into clear causal structure, what happens unforeseen or even unforeseeably is incorporated into clear causal structure, and all causal agency except that of the parts of the action themselves is excluded. Given the temptation to fall into emotionalism or obscurantism, especially the obscurantism connected with traditional Greek piety, which held the workings of fate or chance or other divine powers to be beyond human comprehension, Aristotle's emphasis on *katharsis* no longer seems "extreme." It is the epitome of fourth-century philosophical rationalism, of the "characteristic confidence which it [the *Poetics*] shows in the rational, methodical and objective character of the philosopher's quest" (see Section 3.1 above). It is, in a word, Aristotelian. Just so does he deal with emotional aspects in other contexts, giving them a clear rational structure in the *Ethics* rather than subjecting them to the Platonic invective of beastliness (*therion*, lion, many-headed beast, white and black horse, etc.). Just so does he deal with obscurity, resolving *aporiae* in terms of his own rational distinctions and making even chance (*tychon*) comprehensible.[13]

The definitional achievement of tragedy lies not in denying the emotive content of the action but in making it causally comprehensible. Emotive content and clarity of structure are given together in the definition. Neither is listed as a constitutive part in its own right, and neither is listed as a type of differentia in its own right. As argued above, both must then fall under one of the listed six constitutive parts and under one of the three types of differentiae, and that can only be the action. For the action (*praxeos*) is elucidated as *mythos* in the selective sense of plot-structure, and the emotive content is elucidated as being incorporated into this structure:

> Since the imitation is not only of a complete action but also of actions which are fearsome and pitiful, these come to be most whenever things happen unforeseeably and yet because of one another (ἐπεὶ δὲ οὐ μόνον τελείας ἐστὶ πράξεως ἡ μίμησις ἀλλὰ καὶ φοβερῶν καὶ ἐλεεινῶν, ταῦτα δὲ γίνεται καὶ μάλιστα ὅταν γένηται παρὰ τὴν δόξαν δι᾽ ἄλληλα). (9.1452a1–4)

The "action" (*praxeos*) used in the definition is a constitutive part of tragedy only if its *mimesis* achieves the clarification of its causal structure as incorporating its emotive content, for the above quote explicitly refers back to the wording of the formal definition (cf. 11.1452a38–b1).

The double characterization of the action in the formal definition is in its further elaboration (which occupies chapters 6–14 and several times restates the wording of the definition) shown to be but a single characterization. Chapter 6 elucidates *praxis* as *mythos*, and this is elaborated both structurally and as having emotive content. The beginning of chapter 7 changes the wording of the definition: instead of "of an action which is serious, complete, and has some magnitude" (*praxeos spoudaias kai teleias megethos echouses*), it has "of a complete and whole action having some magnitude" (*teleias kai holes praxeos echouses ti megethos;* 7.1450b24–25). *Spoudaias* drops out as a characterization of the action (at 9.1451b6 it reappears only in the comparative, *spoudaioteron,* marking poetry in general as more serious than history). *Teleias* is elaborated as *holes,* while *megethos echouses* is elaborated as a quantitative property of the *mythos,* its "sufficient limit of length" (7.1450b34–1a15). The *mythos* is elaborated structurally (as a whole and so as a unity in terms of the sequential-causal nexus of its parts, which are themselves actions) and as being of a certain qualitative nature (*poian tina;* 7.1450b21–22). That qualitative nature is the pitiful and fearsome character of the actions of which it consists (*[praxeon] phoberon kai eleeinon;* 9.1452a2–4). This structural-emotive elaboration recurs several times. At 11.1452a36–b3, it is linked particularly with reversal and recognition and good and bad fortune: "But the recognition I have mentioned is the one which is most integral to the plot-structure and its action: for such a combination of recognition and reversal will have pity or fear (and according to our definition, tragedy is the imitation of such actions), since both affliction and prospering will depend on such actions." At 13.1452b30–33, the best tragedy is defined as having a complex structure and as imitating fearsome and pitiful actions: "Since then the structure of the finest tragedy should not be simple but complex and should imitate fearsome and pitiful actions (for this is characteristic of this kind of imitation)." And at 13.1453a18–23, this emotive content is explained as suffering or committing terrible actions: "[T]he finest tragedies are constructed around a few families . . . and others who have suffered or committed terrible actions. The tragedy which is finest according to the standards of the art then consists of this structure." The structural-emotive elaboration of the *mythos* is intracategorial in the category of *ousia.*

This is confirmed by Aristotle's use of categorial contrasts, especially that between *ousia* and *pros ti,* which denies the latter any definitory role. It first appears in chapter 4: "a tragedy . . . judging it both in itself and in relation to audiences . . ." (*he tragodia . . . auto te kath hauto krinai kai pros ta theatra . . .* ; 1449a7–9). The "in itself" is soon after repeated as a tragedy's own nature (*ten hautes physin),* which functions as governing final cause. *Pros ta theatra* drops out of consideration. But in chapter 6 it is explicitly denied any definitory role and indeed any integral connection with poetical *techne:* "but spectacle, while persuasive, is least integral to poetical *techne*" (*he de opsis psychagogikon men, atechnotaton de kai hekista oikeion tes poietikes;* 6.1450b16–18). This is repeated in chapter 7: "But the limit of the length [of the *mythos*] in relation to competitions and perception of audiences is not part of poetical *techne*" (*tou de mekous horos <ho> men pros tous agonas kai ten aisthesin ou tes technes estin;* 7.1451a6–7). Why this careful exclusion of a tragedy's relation to audiences (*pros ti)* from the poetical *techne?*

The reason is the danger that the third differentia, manner of imitation *(hos)*, might be misunderstood. Since it (along with the other two) differentiates the generic nature into specific natures, it must function like an Aristotelian differentia. That means that it must be responsive to the generic nature and cannot contradict it. It must be *oikeion* to the subject genus. But if it were misunderstood as falling into the category of relation *(pros ti)*, it would contradict the generic nature, which is common to all works of art. If a tragedy were defined *pros ta theatra*, it could not simultaneously be defined as falling into the subject genus *mimesis* and so could not be conceptualized as an artistic thing. For artistic *techne* is distinguished from non-artistic *technai* such as house building, medical treatment, and rhetorical speechmaking by what I have called *mimesis* 2, having representational content. Every *techne* is defined by its product or end, none is defined by its means, since a *poiesis*, in contrast to a *praxis*, has a defining *telos* different from and beyond *(heteron kai para)* the process of making. The product of artistic *techne* has representational content, while the products of non-artistic *technai* do not.

Commentators and translators have focused on the content of Aristotle's formal definition of tragedy at the beginning of chapter 6. But prior to that is a consideration of its status and nature. For Aristotle, a formal definition is technical and uses technical terminology, and it is expressed in terms of generic nature and differentiae. Since the generic nature is *mimesis* 2 and the three differentiae are *praxeos*, logoi, and *di' dronton*, these three must be the ways in which *mimesis* is differentiated into *tragike mimesis*. A tragedy is then defined as a product of human *techne* that has tragic representational content. But whatever causal effect it may have on an audience (whether spectator or reader), will not have representational content. An audience's pity or fear or pleasure or *katharsis* are not themselves *mimetic* 2 of anything, any more than a patient's health or a rhetorical audience's belief. If *di' dronton* were misunderstood as falling into the category of *pros ti (pros ta theatra)*, artistic *techne* would be reduced to non-artistic, and the formal definition would cancel itself through an explicit internal contradiction between the generic nature *(mimesis* 2) and a differentia *(di' dronton)*. The same reasoning applies to the "achieving the *katharsis*" *(perainousa ten katharsin)* of the definition.

The danger of such misunderstanding (as the history of exegesis of the *Poetics* testifies) is not negligible, and Aristotle does not neglect it. "In the dramatic mode" *(di' dronton)* is no more to be understood *pros ta theatra* (as falling into the category of *pros ti*) than is its contrasting "in the narrative mode" *(di' apangelias)*. And clearly both have to fall into the same category. When he elucidates its meaning as implying *opseos kosmos* and recognizes *opsis* as one of the six constitutive parts, he is quick to clarify that it is not to be understood *pros ta theatra*. He recognizes its effect on audiences *(psychagogikon)* but denies that this effect functions as a differentia in the subject genus *mimesis*. As falling under the differentia, manner of imitation, and so being an integral part of poetical *techne*, it must differentiate the generic nature itself, it must function as a differentiation of a tragedy's own representational content.

A tragedy's effect on a recipient must be subsequent to its having achieved its own tragic representational content, to its being a *tragike mimesis* in its own right. It cannot be definitory for it. This does not mean that a tragedy, just like anything else, may not causally affect a recipient. But it does mean that its own intrinsic nature is prior to, and hence not definable in terms of, any such effect. *Ousia* enjoys its normal categorial priority to *pros ti*, and its definition is stated in an unqualified manner *(haplos)*. It follows that for Aristotle, an individual tragedy has actual being independently of being performed or experienced by a recipient. By contrast, an individual case of medical treatment or of rhetorical speechmaking has actual being only if and when it is producing a causal effect on a recipient. Aristotle's theory of art thus stands in sharp contrast to any *Rezeptionsästhetik*, but translators and commentators have rarely followed his strict categorial priority of *ousia* to *pros ti* consistently.

The distinction between what pertains to poetical *techne* in itself *(kath hauten)* and what pertains to it only accidentally *(kata symbebekos)* is established at the generic level and is grounded in the generic definition of art as *mimesis* 2. It is not established at the specific level, and so the focus of the scholarly discussion on what is specifically tragic misses the right level. This makes it difficult if not impossible to resolve the question whether a tragedy is defined in the category of *ousia* or in that of *pros ti*. (Nothing, for Aristotle, could be defined in both simultaneously!) At the beginning of chapter 25 (1460b6–32) he restates the distinction at the generic level and then uses it to resolve *aporiai* formulated by others. An artist is generically a *mimeticist:* "[A]n artist is one who imitates" *(esti mimetes ho poietes; 25.1460b8;* cf. *1.1447b13–23; 9.1451b28–29).* Hence, the standards of correctness that pertain to artistic *techne* in itself are also determined at the generic level, and a mistake that violates them does so because the artist is doing something "non-*mimetically*" *(amimetos; 25.1460b32).* The differentiae of tragedy, like those of any other species of art, must function *mimetos*. They cannot do so in the category of *pros ti*, since the experience of an audience that is produced by a tragedy is not itself *mimetic* of anything. Hence the categorial priority of *ousia* is confirmed.

3.1.4 Immanent Causal Form-Matter Constitution in the Category of Ousia

As argued in Section 1.2.4 above, the reason for the categorial priority of *ousia* is that it alone is causally constituted by immanent form and matter. These are themselves *ousiai*. Aristotle therefore gives two different accounts *(logoi)* of an *ousia*, one definitional and the other functional (see Section 2.3 above). The definitional account sets out the descriptive content of an *ousia's* essential nature (genus-differentiae), while the functional account sets out how form and matter causally constitute the *ousia*. It is functional in Aristotle's, not in our sense. We understand a functional account as extrinsic and relational, setting out a thing's causal effect on another thing. That, for Aristotle, is transeunt efficient causality. He understands a functional account as intrinsic, setting out the constitutive functioning of a thing's form and matter. That, for him, is immanent formal-final and material causality. It is the latter which grounds and explains the categorial priority of *ousia*.[14]

An *ousia* is in its own intrinsic being prior to any efficient causality it may exert extrinsically on other things, and hence no extrinsic effect can enter either into its essential definitional or functional account. Conversely, anything whose essential definitional or functional account includes such an extrinsic effect, is not an *ousia*. I have argued that a tragedy's definitional account includes no such effect, and I shall now argue that its functional account does not either.

Its functional account is not stated in the *Poetics* in terms of form *(energeia)* and matter *(dynamis)*. But it is implicitly present in the rank-ordering of the six constitutive parts, in their functional characterization, and in explicit analogies.

The rank-ordering in chapter 6 could easily be misunderstood as indicating differences of degree in the importance of the six parts rather than differences in type of constitutive causality. Aristotle is aware that his normal practice of analyzing a definitional account in terms of such parts is apt to be misunderstood in just that way. For differences of degree presuppose that all the constitutive parts are of the same type, have the same mode of being, and function in terms of the same type of constitutive causality. This misunderstanding leads to the *aporia* of how such parts can constitute a real substantial unity:

> To return to the difficulty *(aporias)* which has been stated with respect both to definitions *(horismous)* and to numbers, what is the cause of their unity? For in the case of all things which have several parts *(mere)* and where the totality *(to pan)* is not like a heap *(soros)* but the whole is something beyond the parts *(ti to holon para ta moria)*, there is a cause *(ti aition)*. (*Met.* VIII. 1045a7–10)

Since the unity of a definition derives from the real unity of what is being defined, the same *aporia* recurs:

> And a definition is an account which is one *(logos estin heis)* not by being connected together, like the *Iliad*, but by being the definition of something that is one *(toi henos einai)*. What then is that which makes man one *(ti oun estin ho poiei hen ton anthropon)*, and through what *(dia ti)* is he one rather than many, e.g., both animal and biped *(to te zoon kai to dipoun)?* (*Met.* VIII. 1045a12–15)

The misunderstanding engendered by the language of parts is so ubiquitous that nobody except Aristotle can resolve the *aporia*: "Clearly, then, people who proceed thus in their accustomed manner of defining and speaking, cannot explain and solve the *aporia*" (*Met.* VIII. 1045a20–22). Only Aristotle can resolve it, as usual by means of a conceptual distinction which he introduces:

> But if, as we say, one part is matter *(hyle)* and another is form *(morphe)*, and the matter is potentially *(dynamei)* while the form is actually *(energeiai)*, the question will no longer be thought to be an *aporia*. (*Met.* VIII. 1045a23–25; cf. 1045a29)

The conceptual distinction, which resolves the *aporia* and allows us to understand a definitional account as a real substantial unity of its constitutive parts, is the distinction between potentiality and actuality as modes of being. Not all the parts can have the same mode of being on pain of either reducing the definitional account to something like a heap *(soros;* i.e., a mere summative aggregate of its parts) or of engendering an infinite regress *(eis apeiron badieitai; Met.* VII. 17). One of the parts must have being in the mode of actuality *(einai energeiai)*, the others in the mode of potentiality *(einai dynamei)*. The one that has being in the mode of actuality functions as formal cause *(morphe, eidos)*, the others function as aspects of the material cause *(hyle)*. The formal cause actualizes all aspects of the material cause and so is the cause *(aition)* that "makes one out of many" *(to poioun hen ek pollon)*. It is the *ousia*, the cause of the thing's being *(aition tou einai)*. It is not itself an element but something else *(heteron ti)*, the primary cause of the thing's being *(aition proton tou einai)*, its essential nature *(physis)*, its *arche* (see *Met.* VII. 17 and VIII. 3). In just this manner does the soul function as *ousia* and *energeia* of its body (*Met.* VIII. 1043a35–36). And generally, formal and final cause coincide (cf. *Physics* II).

It is clear that this, in contrast to a definition that merely states genus and differentiae, is a functional account. Its applicability to the unity of a complex definition results from Aristotle's use of matter and potentiality in several senses and on different levels. They designate not only physical but also intelligible matter and potentiality, so that these concepts are applicable to the solution of the *aporia* of substantial unity. That *aporia* immediately poses itself because Aristotle defines a tragedy as being very complex indeed. Its formal definition contains the generic nature and three types of differentiae, and this complexity is increased when he elucidates the meaning or descriptive content of these differentiae as implying six constitutive parts. What can save such a complex thing from being, and so being defined as, a mere heap *(soros)*, a mere summative aggregate of all these parts? What can make a *tragike mimesis* be a genuine specific nature, which is more than the sum of its parts?

Only a distinction of type between one of these parts and the others, a distinction in mode of being, a distinction in type of constitutive causality. One of the six parts must be something else *(heteron ti)*, it must be actuality *(energeia)*, it must function as formal-final cause *(telos, eidos)*, as the primary cause of the being of the tragedy *(aition proton tou einai)*, as its *arche*. This part must, in short, function analogously to the soul of a living animal.

Aristotle does not explicitly state the *aporia* of substantial unity at the end of his definitional account in chapter 6 *(kai para tauta ouden;* 6.1450a12), but he immediately proceeds to give a functional account which singles one of the six constitutive parts, the *mythos,* out for the kind of primacy that alone can resolve the *aporia.* He remains almost exclusively focused on this part until the end of chapter 14 (chapter 12 is different). This is the same part that is also singled out in the formal definition, where the achievement of tragedy is said to be the causal-structural clarification of the action with its emotive content.

The priority of the *mythos* over the other five parts is unmistakable and is explicitly and repeatedly present in the text. Almost immediately after the enumeration that ends the definitional account (6.1450a12), Aristotle rank-orders them from first to sixth. He offers reasons for this ranking, which takes up all the rest of chapter 6, actually its largest part. The wording and the reasons give priority to the *mythos* by intrinsic reference to its role within the tragedy itself, which is subsequently confirmed by reference to historical and current observed facts, including a tragedy's transeunt effect on an audience.

The wording of the ranking in chapter 6: the *mythos* is the most important of the six parts *(megiston de touton;* 6.1450a15). It is the final cause of the tragedy *(telos tes tragodias;* 6.1450a22–23). It is indispensable for a tragedy *(aneu men praxeos ouk an genoito tragodia;* 6.1450a23–24). It is the work of the tragedy *(tes tragodias ergon;* 6.1450a30–31).[15] It is the *arche* of the tragedy which functions analogously to a soul *(arche men kai hoion psyche ho mythos tes tragodias;* 6.1450a38–39). Chapter 7 adds that the *mythos* is first and most important (*kai proton kai megiston tes tragodias;* 7.1450b23). Chapter 9 calls the poet a maker of *mythoi* rather than of verses (*ton poieten mallon ton mython einai dei poieten e ton metron;* 9.1451b27–28). Chapter 17 advises him to begin by laying out the general structure of the *mythos* (*poiounta ektithesthai katholou, eith . . . ;* 17.1455b1). And chapter 18 sees tragedies as being the same or different in terms of their *mythos* (*dikaion de kai tragodian allen kai ten auten legein oudeni hos toi mythoi;* 18.1456a7–8).

The priority of the *mythos* (*megiston, telos, aneu ouk tragodia, ergon, arche hoion psyche, proton*) is clearly one of type, not merely of degree. And it is just as clearly intrinsic functional priority. For this is the technical terminology by which Aristotle normally singles out the formal-final cause, the actuality (*energeia*) of a thing, which functions as actualization of the constitutive material cause or potentiality (*dynamis*). It is applied only to the *mythos*, not to any of the other constitutive parts. And it is applied to the entire *mythos*, not to any one of its parts or aspects. The *mythos* as a whole is the intrinsic *telos* of a tragedy.[16] A tragedy, like anything else, has only one constitutive *telos*, only one part that functions intrinsically analogously to the way the soul functions within a living animal. All attempts to find multiple definitory *tele* in Aristotle's account are incompatible with the wording by which he singles the *mythos* out for constitutive priority.[17] It follows that the poet is most of all a maker of a *mythos*, that he should begin with it, and that tragedies should be compared essentially in terms of it.

Aristotle justifies the priority of the *mythos* by explicit backward reference to the wording of the formal definition at the beginning of chapter 6 (*estin oun tragodia mimesis praxeos*): the mythos is the greatest (*megiston*) of all the constitutive parts: "For a tragedy is an imitation not of human beings but of actions and life" (*he gar tragodia mimesis estin ouk anthropon alla praxeon kai biou;* 6.1450a16–17).[18] "Tragedies do not include actions in order to imitate characters, but they include characters for the sake of the actions" (οὔκουν ὅπως τὰ ἤθη μιμήσωνται πράττουσιν, ἀλλὰ τὰ ἤθη συμπεριλαμβάνουσιν διὰ τὰς πράξεις; 6.1450a20–22). "Hence the events and the *mythos* are the final cause of the tragedy, but the final cause is most important of all" (ὥστε τὰ πράγματα καὶ ὁ μῦθος τέλος τῆς τραγῳδίας, τὸ δὲ τέλος μέγιστον ἁπάντων; 6.1450a22–23). Here, as elsewhere in the text, Aristotle safeguards the intrinsic priority of the *mythos* most carefully against the possible misunderstanding that the inner constitution of a tragedy mirrors that of human life. In life, the human agent is prior because he is the *ousia* and responsible cause (*aition*) of his actions, but in a tragedy the action is prior because it functions as first principle analogously to the soul of an animal. The functional account explains the wording of the formal definition and of its elucidation

(6.1450b3–4). A tragedy is defined as a *mimesis praxeos*, i.e., the *mythos* has constitutive primacy. It is that primacy that constitutes the new specific nature, the *tragike mimesis*. Aristotle's severely selective emphasis on *mythos* spells out the generic distance between life and art.

The intrinsic primacy of the *mythos* is subsequently confirmed in chapter 6 by extrinsic reference to facts of observation *(ta ginomena)*. These are, as usual, not part of the argument itself but subsequent confirmation of its result, normally introduced by "moreover" *(eti)*, "following these" *(pros toutois)*, and "sign" *(semeion)*. They include historical and current facts as well as a tragedy's effect on audiences and success in the theatre. Aristotle lists a fair number: the primary status of the *mythos* is confirmed by the fact that characters *(ethe)* are generally deficient in tragedies and particularly so in most recent ones, that well-made characters and articulated rationality *(dianoia)* and language *(lexis)* are not sufficient to make a good tragedy, that even in terms of effect on audiences the *mythos* is most powerful, that poetic novices can achieve precision in language and characters before they achieve it in *mythos*, that almost all early poets were better at language and characters than at *mythos*. These are signs of the primacy of the *mythos (semeia)*, because what is earlier in development is posterior in constitutive importance, widespread deficiency in secondary aspects does not debar works from counting as tragedies, and in addition *(pros de toutois)* a tragedy has a greater causal effect on audiences in terms of its *mythos* than in terms of its other five parts. The end of chapter 6, which ranks spectacle *(opsis)* in sixth place despite its admitted effect on audiences, confirms that effect on audiences *(psychagogei* occurs both with respect to *mythos* and to *opsis* in the text) is only a sign, not itself constitutive of a tragedy's essential nature.

The other five constitutive parts are designated as being of secondary intrinsic status by contrast with the primary status of the *mythos*, and this designation is explicitly present in the text in its wording, in the reasons given, and in subsequent confirmation by signs *(semeia)*. The same texts often embody the contrast, so that citing them with respect to both the primary and the secondary would involve considerable overlap. It is clear that the secondary status of the other five parts is functional: they do not function within the tragedy in the same way as the *mythos*, they function in a way that is secondary. Their rank-ordering from second to sixth is a further refinement within their shared secondary functional status. If the *mythos* functions analogously to the soul of a living animal, then they must function analogously to its body. If the *mythos* functions as *arche*, then they are those aspects of a tragedy over which the *mythos* exercises its *arche*-function. An Aristotelian functional account requires correlatives: what is primary requires what is secondary, and the rule of an *arche* is impossible without something that is subject to that rule. Throughout this account, Aristotle is most concerned to subject characters *(ethe)* to the rule of the *mythos*.[19]

Chapter 6 argues for the secondary status of the other five constitutive parts by explicit reference back to the wording of the formal definition *(estin oun tragodia mimesis praxeos)*, and this reference remains the basic premise throughout the following chapters. Else has recognized that their secondary status is argued for, and he goes so far as to say that it is deduced from the definition. He, however, believes that it is deduced from the differentia manner of imitation *(hos, di' dronton)*, while I believe that it is deduced from the differentia objects of imitation *(ha, praxeos)*, and indeed from *praxis* defined as *mythos*.[20]

The argument proceeds as follows: chapter 6 establishes the primacy of the *mythos*. Chapter 7 opens by using that primacy as the reason for the following extensive discussion of what the *mythos* should be like: "Given these distinctions, let us next say what the structure of events should be like, since it is the first and most important part of the tragedy" (Διωρισμένων δὲ τούτων, λέγωμεν μετὰ ταῦτα ποίαν τινὰ δεῖ τὴν σύστασιν εἶναι τῶν πραγμάτων, ἐπειδὴ τοῦτο καὶ πρῶτον καὶ μέγιστον τῆς τραγῳδίας ἐστίν; 7.1450b21–23). What the *mythos* should be like *(poian tina dei einai)* is subsequently characterized in two ways, structurally as a whole *(holon)* and emotively as pitiful and fearsome *(eleeinon kai phoberon)*, until this account is closed in the last sentence of chapter 14: "Let this then suffice concerning the structure of events and what the *mythoi* should be like" (περὶ μὲν οὖν τῆς τῶν πραγμάτων συστάσεως καὶ ποίους τινὰς εἶναι δεῖ τοὺς μύθους εἴρηται ἱκανῶς; 14.1454a13–15).

The secondary status of the other five constitutive parts is argued for first on the basis of the structural characterization of the *mythos*, then on the basis of its emotive characterization. It may be noted in passing that what the *mythos* should be like is discussed even in the chapters following chapter 14, and that Aristotle calls his account in chapters 7–14 "sufficient" *(hikanos)*, in contrast to Halliwell's "extreme" and Else's "obsession." It may also be worth noting that he usually devotes much more discussion to the part of a thing that functions as *arche* analogously to the soul of a living animal, i.e., to its formal-final constitutive cause, than to those parts that function as its correlative material cause. The functional account of the *Poetics* is quite in keeping with his normal practice.

The structural argument begins with the second sentence of chapter 7: "We have already laid down that tragedy is an imitation of an action which is complete, whole, and has some magnitude" (7.1450b23–25). Of these characteristics of the action, "whole" *(holes)* carries the burden of the argument. It is immediately defined: "A whole is what has beginning and middle and end" *(holon de estin to echon archen kai meson kai teleuten;*

7.1450b26–27). These three terms are immediately defined: "A beginning is what itself is not after something else by necessity *(ex anankes)* but after which something else is or comes to be naturally *(pephyken)*. An end by contrast is what itself is naturally *(pephyken)* after something else by necessity or for the most part *(e ex anankes e hos epi to poly)*, but after which there is nothing else. Middle is what both itself is after something else and after which there is something else" (7.1450b27–31). Aristotle draws the conclusion that a well-constructed *mythos* is therefore *(ara)* a whole whose beginning and end are not arbitrary *(etychen)* but in accordance with the above definitions.

Chapter 8 presents this wholeness as the unity of the *mythos*, what makes it one *(heis)*. Such unity is necessary if there is to be a tragedy. For tragedy can be a specific nature within the subject genus imitation *(mimesis* 2) only if it is one, a single *mimesis* *(mia mimesis;* 8.1451a30–31). This is generally true of all specific natures within the genus *mimesis* *(kathaper kai en tais allais mimetikais;* 8.1451a30), and it is of course true of any specific nature whatever. But since the generic nature imitation *(mimesis* 2) just means having representational content, a specific nature within it can be one only by being of one object *(he mia mimesis henos estin)*. Tragic imitation *(tragike mimesis)* can be a genuine specific nature only if it is the imitation of an object that is one, and since it has been defined as the imitation of an action *(praxeos mimesis)*, its object must be an action that is one in the sense of being a whole. For the action is complex, consisting of parts, and complex unity is wholeness:

> Just as in the other mimetic arts a single imitation is of
> a single object, so it is also necessary that the *mythos,*
> since it is the imitation of an action, is of a single action
> which is a whole . . . (χρὴ οὖν, καθάπερ καὶ ἐν ταῖς ἄλλαις
> μιμητικαῖς ἡ μία μίμησις ἑνός ἐστιν, οὕτω καὶ τὸν μῦθον,
> ἐπεὶ πράξεως μίμησίς ἐστι, μιᾶς τε εἶναι καὶ ταύτης ὅλης).
> (8.1451a30–32)

Aristotle ends the chapter by setting breathtakingly stringent standards for the structural wholeness of the parts of the action (8.1451a32–35).

This structural requirement of wholeness of the action relegates the protagonist who acts to secondary status, since he cannot provide the necessary wholeness:

> The *mythos* is one, not as some people think, whenever
> it is about one person . . . the actions of a single person
> are many, out of which no single action comes to be

(Μῦθος δ' ἐστὶν εἷς οὐχ ὥσπερ τινὲς οἴονται ἐὰν περὶ
ἕνα ᾖ. . . πράξεις ἑνὸς πολλαί εἰσιν, ἐξ ὧν μία οὐδεμία
γίνεται πρᾶξις). (8.1451a16–19)

That is why Homer structured the *Odyssey* and the *Iliad* around a single
action, which is whole in the sense defined above (. . . περὶ μίαν πρᾶξιν
οἵαν λέγομεν τὴν ᾿Οδύσσειαν συνέστησεν, ὁμοίως δὲ καὶ τὴν ᾿Ιλιάδα;
8.1451a28–30). Since the protagonist who acts is present in the tragedy in
terms of the two constitutive parts, characters *(ethe)* and articulated rationality *(dianoia)*, these are relegated to secondary status: they cannot provide the necessary unity of the action.

The unity of the action lies in two aspects. Since it has to be a single
complex action, all the parts of which it consists must themselves be
actions. For otherwise it would be a complex whole consisting of actions
and of some other parts. The beginning and middle and end must therefore be actions. And what connects these actions into one whole action
must be a very strong bond of unity, if it is to be a genuine whole and
not merely a sum or aggregate of parts. Chapter 7 characterizes this bond
of unity as being a sequence by necessity *(ex anankes)*, naturally *(pephyken)*,
for the most part *(epi to poly)*. The end of chapter 8 makes it stringently
precise: "and its parts should be so constructed out of events that the
displacement or removal of any one of them will distort and disjoint the
work's wholeness" (καὶ τὰ μέρη συνεστάναι τῶν πραγμάτων οὕτως ὥστε
μετατιθεμένου τινὸς μέρους ἢ ἀφαιρουμένου διαφέρεσθαι καὶ κινεῖσθαι
τὸ ὅλον). The end of chapter 10 sums up that it must be causal, not
merely sequential *(tade dia tade)*. The action-causality involved here is
clearly efficient causality.

The unity of tragedy as a specific nature, then, requires the functional isolation of the action on its own level. Both the parts of which it
consists and the causal bonds of unity between these parts lie on the
level of action. All other constitutive parts of the tragedy must be excluded from this level. It is this self-contained isolation that enables the
action to function analogously to the soul of a living animal and so to
function with the constitutive primacy of an immanent formal-final cause.
The exclusion of the other five parts from the action and their relegation
to secondary functional status are the price a tragedy has to pay for
having a genuine specific nature of its own *(ten hautes physin; 4.1449a15)*.

Perhaps now it is clearer why Aristotle introduces *katharsis* into the
formal definition of tragedy and designates it as what a tragedy must
achieve. Certainly *katharsis* can readily be understood as the clarity of the
action's causal structure in the sense that all irrational, fortuitous, and
personalized aspects must be excluded from it. But the achievement of
the action's isolation on its own level, which enables it to be one action

of the type the tragedy requires in order to be itself one, the establishment of its functional primacy, can be understood as a more profound compositional clearing. For it is this that transforms the action and with it the tragedy into a genuine unity, which is more than the sum of its parts. To achieve this *katharsis* of the action is fundamentally the poet's task. He is a maker of *mythoi* more than of any of the other constitutive parts, because what he has to make is not just the structure of an action, but a structure that enables the action to function as compositional principle of the tragedy. For in art, the compositional principle functions analogously to the soul in a living animal. Aristotle uses the same term, *synistanai*, for the primacy of the action that he uses for the primacy of the soul in his biological treatises. *Katharsis* as compositional clearing meets the Aristotelian connotation of the word, namely, achieving what belongs to the *physis* of a tragedy *(ten hautes physin)*.[21]

The poet's making *(poiein)*, his *poiesis* or *techne*, is then indeed the creation of something new, of something that is not already there in life. Neither the structural wholeness of the action nor its constitutive functioning as compositional principle are already there in life, to be found or copied. Chapter 8 sets out the contrasting structures of life and of art. In life, actions are focused on the agent just like his other accidents, indeed, an individual agent's actions are themselves among his accidents in the secondary category of doing *(poiein)*. They are many and have no unity on their own level, their only unity being derived from the agent. Halliwell therefore translates the structure of life as "centring on an individual." Nor does an action function as the *arche* and soul of an individual human being, since the human soul is his formal-final cause. In life, the agent is prior to the action.[22]

Art is impossible if it copies this structure, despite the mistaken belief *(hamartanein)* of "some people" *(tines oiontai)* and many poets that art should or could be a mirror of life in this sense. Homer, as usual, knew better. Art, whose products have a new generic and new specific natures, must have a new structure. That structure must be focused on the action. The action must be prior to the agent. While life is focused on an individual *(peri hena)*, art is focused on an action *(peri mian praxin)*. The artist produces this profound refocusing.

Nor is focusing on the action optional in the sense that something else could function as a tragedy's compositional principle. A formal Aristotelian definition has a highly prescriptive status. A tragedy is defined as the imitation of an action because that is what it is, its *ti esti*. Without an action in this functional role, there could no more be a tragedy than there could be a living animal without its soul in the analogous functional role. The reason is not simply that Aristotle is not an easygoing modern pluralist, let alone a relativist. The idea of unbounded artistic freedom would have struck him as anarchic, not as creative. The reason is rather that the compositional principle as formal-final cause is actuality, while the other five parts are potentiality. The action is actuality in the sense that the distinctive nature of the tragic is present in it, that it is intrinsically and in its own right tragic. The other five parts are potentiality in the sense that the distinctive nature of the tragic is not actually present in any of them, that none of them is intrinsically and in its own right tragic. Aristotle's definition of tragedy implies not only that this is so but that this is necessarily so. The reason for this is given in the dual structural-emotive characterization of the action as clear in its causal structure and as consisting of actions that are pitiful and fearsome. The combination of such structural wholeness with such emotive content is the achievement of the tragic. This achievement must lie in the action, for it is possible for a well-constructed *mythos* to be a genuine whole that is pitiful and fearsome, but it is not possible for characters *(ethe)*, articulated rationality *(dianoia)*, language *(logos)*, verse *(melopoiia)*, or spectacle *(opsis)* to be so. Our modern way of speaking of "tragic heroes," "tragic characters," "tragic emotions," is not compatible with Aristotle's priority of the action. For the action is what is primarily tragic, while the other five parts are so secondarily in the sense that they must be chosen by the playwright so as to be suitable or potentially tragic. This potentiality can then be actualized by the action. The primary status of the action and the secondary status of the other five constitutive parts is an instance of the priority of actuality to potentiality, analogous to the priority of soul to body.

Chapter 9 links this priority of the action explicitly with the poet's status as an imitator:

> It is therefore clear that the poet should be the maker of plot-structures more than of verses, in as far as his status as poet depends on imitation, and he imitates actions (δῆλον οὖν ἐκ τούτων ὅτι τὸν ποιητὴν μᾶλλον τῶν μύθων εἶναι δεῖ ποιητὴν ἢ τῶν μέτρων, ὅσῳ ποιητὴς κατὰ τὴν μίμησίν ἐστιν, μιμεῖται δὲ τὰς πράξεις). (9.1451b27–29)

The *poietes-mimetes* link recurs several times in the *Poetics*, since art is generically defined as imitation *(mimesis* 2). But the above link of action as the object of imitation with the poet's status as an imitator suggests that the priority of the action is necessary for all art, that anything can be a work of art only if it is the imitation of an action. The priority of the action is then required not only specifically for tragedy but generically for art as such. This link is suggested, but the text does not argue it explicitly for all other species of art, though it does for tragedy, epic, and comedy.

The emotive (in contrast to the structural) argument for the secondary status of the other five constitutive parts begins in chapter 9 with an explicit reference back to the formal definition of tragedy: "Since tragedy is the imitation not only of a complete action but also of fearsome and pitiful actions," (*epei de ou monon teleias esti praxeos he mimesis alla kai phoberon kai eleeinon*; 9.1452a1–3). Here it is taken for granted that the action is characterized both structurally (*teleias*) and emotively (*phoberon kai eleeinon*) in the formal definition. For "fearsome" and "pitiful," which here occur in a justifying secondary clause (*epei*), have previously occurred only in the formal definition of tragedy in chapter 6. Halliwell translates so as to make them characteristics of the action: "Since tragic mimesis portrays not just a whole action, but events which are fearful and pitiful."[23] Aristotle immediately goes on to incorporate the emotive content in the action's structure: "But these actions arise best when they come about contrary to expectation yet caused by each other" (*tauta de ginetai kai malista hotan genetai para ten doxan di' allela*; 9.1452a3–4). "These actions" (*tauta*) and "each other" (*allela*) refer back to "fearsome and pitiful actions" (*phoberon kai eleeinon*), so that actions and afflictions that have the emotive content of being fearsome and pitiful are said to arise best within the causal-sequential structure, in which the wholeness and unity of the action consists.

This emotive content is tragic only within this structure, so that the distinctive nature of the tragic (*to tragikon*) is found only when the pitiful and fearsome occur together with the action's structural wholeness. For the tragic to arise, it is not sufficient that the actions or events are afflictions (*pathemata*), that they are terrible (*deina*), destructive or painful (*phthartika e odynera*), or pitiful and fearsome. That alone does not make them tragic, for there are pitiful and fearsome events in life, and life is not tragic for Aristotle. It is the causal agency of the actions themselves, unforeseen and yet by necessity or probability, that engenders the specifically tragic emotive content. *Pathemata* become tragic only in terms of this impersonal causal agency. That is why life, which chapter 8 had characterized as focused on the agent (*peri hena*), is not tragic and why tragedy must be focused on the action (*peri mian praxin*) in order to be so. The impersonal causal agency of the action must be cleansed of all personal agency, whether of human beings or divinities. The transformation of *pathemata* into tragic *pathemata* is the achievement of tragedy. "Best" (*malista*) does not mean that the tragic can also come to be some other way, but rather refers to a strong juxtaposition of "contrary to expectation" and "caused by each other," which admits of degrees.

Chapters 10 and 11 designate reversal (*peripeteia*) and recognition (*anagnorisis*) as parts (*mere*) of the action (*mythou*) and tie them into its causal structure (*tauta de dei ginesthai ex autes tes systaseos tou mythou;*

10.1452a18–19). Chapter 11, again referring back to the formal definition of tragedy, incorporates the tragic emotive content into this structure:

> But recognition is finest when it comes about at the same time as reversal. . . . But the recognition I have mentioned is the one which is most integral to the plot-structure and the action. For such recognition and reversal will have pity or fear (tragedy is on our definition the imitation of actions of this kind), since also faring ill and faring well will befall when such actions occur (καλλίστη δὲ ἀναγνώρισις, ὅταν ἅμα περιπετείᾳ γένηται . . . ἀλλ᾽ ἡ μάλιστα τοῦ μύθου καὶ ἡ μάλιστα τῆς πράξεως ἡ εἰρημένη ἐστίν· ἡ γὰρ τοιαύτη ἀναγνώρισις καὶ περιπέτεια ἢ ἔλεον ἕξει ἢ φόβον [οἵων πράξεων ἡ τραγῳδία μίμησις ὑπόκειται], ἐπειδὴ καὶ τὸ ἀτυχεῖν καὶ τὸ εὐτυχεῖν ἐπὶ τῶν τοιούτων συμβήσεται). (11.1452a32–b3)

The reference back to the definition "actions of this kind" (hoion praxeon) implies that tragedy had been defined as the imitation of an action whose emotive content is incorporated into its structure. Chapter 11 focuses particularly on the action's change of fortune, which as integral to the plot-structure will have (hexei) the specifically tragic emotive content, so that good or ill fortune will befall (symbesetai) when such actions occur (epi ton toiouton), i.e., good or ill fortune will befall tragically. The future indicatives are parallel, both refer to the action, and both link the action's structure with its emotive content. Aristotle often uses the future indicative in this emphatic manner.[24]

Chapter 13 uses the same structural-emotive characterization of the action as the premise from which the suitability of characters (ethe) is deduced:

> Since then the structure of the finest tragedy should be not simple but complex and imitative of fearsome and pitiful actions (for this is the distinctive feature of such an imitation), it is first of all clear that . . . (ἐπειδὴ οὖν δεῖ τὴν σύνθεσιν εἶναι τῆς καλλίστης τραγῳδίας μὴ ἁπλῆν ἀλλὰ πεπλεγμένην καὶ ταύτην φοβερῶν καὶ ἐλεεινῶν εἶναι μιμητικήν [τοῦτο γὰρ ἴδιον τῆς τοιαύτης μιμήσεώς ἐστιν], πρῶτον μὲν δῆλον ὅτι . . .). (9.1452b30–34)

The structural-emotive nature of the action is prior and normative for the suitability of ethe, it is the given, the constant reference by which suitable ethe are chosen. This marks the ethe as posterior and derivative, as having secondary status. For they are not chosen independently, by criteria intrinsic to themselves. They are not tragic in their own right but only inasfar as they are suitable to the tragic action. For tragedy is not the imitation of *ethe* but of *praxis*. What is true of *ethe* will pertain to the other four secondary constitutive parts as well. Since *(epeide)* the action must be intrinsically tragic, it follows that *ethe* must be matched to it. Only thus will they not detract from or counteract the functioning of the action as compositional principle of the tragedy.

What clearly follows *(proton men delon hoti)* is that the best character in life and the best character in a tragedy are not the same. In life the best character is the ethically perfect man, in tragedy he is not. Ethical and tragic criteria diverge, life and art are judged by different standards. In art, the ethical dimension is subordinate and so secondary. Standards and criteria are not transferable from one subject genus to another. The ethically best characters in life are judged to be so by the standard of human excellence *(arete)*, the tragically best characters are judged to be so by the standard of tragic excellence *(tes kallistes tragodias)*. Both standards are intrinsic, human excellence to a human being, tragic excellence to a tragedy. Even bad characters are justified in a tragedy if artistically necessary (cf. 15.1454a28–29; 25.1461b19–21).

The tragically best character is between *(metaxy)* ethical goodness and badness, but on the good rather than on the bad side. Aristotle here for the first time in the text expands the notion of structure *(systasis)* beyond *mythos (systasis pragmaton)* to encompass *ethe*, using it now to designate a pattern that consists of an ethical character matched to a certain change of fortune. Most of these patterns are rejected, one is retained. The rejected ones are: good men changing from good to bad fortune, bad men changing from bad to good fortune, bad men changing from good to bad fortune. The one that is retained is: a middling character changing from good to bad fortune.

The first three patterns are rejected because they are not pitiful and fearsome and so not tragic. Their matching of ethical character to action is faulty. The fault lies in the characters' being too strongly marked in ethical terms, so that the focus shifts away from the action to the ethical dimension, which interferes with the functioning of the action as compositional principle. For no strongly marked ethical character is suitable to tragic action at all, it is not merely a question of matching the right character to the right change of fortune. The goodness of a good man *(epieikeis andras)*, when surpassing *(diapheron)*, cannot be matched to any tragic change of fortune. The badness of bad men *(tous mochtherous)*, when surpassing (*kakian* and *mochtherian* are strong terms for Aristotle), cannot be matched to any tragic change of fortune. The reason is that strongly marked ethical character has too much weight and so resists the artistic subordination to the action. Life with its ethical standards and criteria intrudes into art and counteracts artistic standards and criteria. Personal causal agency *(dia kakian kai mochtherian)* disrupts the impersonal causal agency of the action and so its wholeness. This is so whether the agent is ethically good or bad. Such patterns are not tragic because they are too close to the "centring on an individual" (Halliwell's translation of *peri hena*), which chapter 8 had rejected in favour of "focusing on a single action" *(peri mian praxin)*. Focusing on an agent is the structure of ethical life, while focusing on the action is the structure of art. The rejected patterns are not artistic.

The only suitable ethical character is therefore a middling one *(metaxy)*, who exerts no personal causal agency. The error *(hamartia)*, which does play a causal role *(di' hamartian)*, is neither linked with moral character *(ethos)* nor with articulated rationality *(dianoia)*, but is itself an action and so part of the *mythos*. Only thus can the wholeness and unity of the action be preserved. In life the agent with his moral character has a causal role in being the responsible principle of his action *(aition)*, in art he does not. *Hamartia*, as Else has convincingly argued, is the counterpart of recognition *(anagnorisis)* and so part of the action, it is a failure of recognition.[25] The secondary status of *ethe* lies most poignantly in their exclusion from a causal role.

It bears repeating that the *ethe* are never by themselves or in their own right tragic, so that one cannot speak of tragic characters but only of tragic action-character patterns. The text is quite clear on this point. The "this" *(touto)* at 13.1452b36 and at 13.1452b37 refer back to the expanded structure as a whole, as does "such a structure" *(he toiaute systasis)* at 13.1453a3. The entire argument from "since" *(epeide)* at 13.1452b30 on is objective, focused on this structure and characterizing it as being either pitiful and fearsome or merely disgusting *(miaron)* or moving *(philanthropon):* "For such a structure would have the moving but neither pity nor fear . . . so that what happens will be neither pitiful nor fearsome" (τὸ μὲν γὰρ φιλάνθρωπον ἔχοι ἂν ἡ τοιαύτη σύστασις ἀλλ᾽ οὔτε ἔλεον οὔτε φόβον . . . ὥστε οὔτε ἐλεεινὸν οὔτε φοβερὸν ἔσται τὸ συμβαῖνον; 13.1453a2–7). The argument is summed up and concluded with the same objective focus on this structure itself:

> A fine plot-structure must therefore be single rather than double, as some people think, and it must change not from bad to good fortune but on the contrary from good to bad fortune, not because of badness of character but because of a significant failure of recognition, either of a character such as has been described or of one who is better rather than worse. (13.1453a12–17)

Only after the argument is completed, does Aristotle add empirical confirmation in terms of considerations extrinsic to the tragedy. It is, as often in the *Poetics*, introduced as a sign: "A sign of this is what actually happens" (*semeion de kai to gignomenon;* 13.1453a17). It includes historical facts, audience reaction, success on the stage and in competitions. The latter are, however, immediately marked as unreliable signs because a recipient's reaction and success on the stage and in competitions are very often seriously misleading. The fact that a recipient experiences pleasure (or pity and fear) is no proof that a tragedy is fine. Such signs are therefore not part of Aristotle's argument and *a fortiori* not of his definition of tragedy.

Chapters 13 and 14, having shown the unreliability of these signs, establish prescriptive criteria (*dei*) for appropriate audience reaction (an audience can be a reader). Appropriate pleasure (or pity and fear) will be a reliable sign. But what makes it appropriate? Only the understanding of the objectively tragic nature of tragedy (cf. *ten hautes physin;* 4.1449a15). Appropriate audience reaction is cognitive even in its emotional aspects, taking pleasure in what is objectively pleasant, feeling pity and fear for what is objectively pitiful and fearsome. It is appropriate because it is rational, because its subjective aspect is objectively grounded in a cognitive object. Rational subjective pleasure is a reliable sign, because it truly derives from the tragedy (*apo tes tragodias),* arises out of the tragic action (*ek ton symbainonton),* belongs to the tragedy's own household (*oikeian),* in the sense that the tragedy itself causes it in a recipient. Even so, it is only a sign, since its cognitive content is determined by its object, the tragedy itself. Euripides' tragedies are veridically seen to be most tragic (*tragikotatai phainontai),* because they are most tragic in their own intrinsic being, according to the highest standard of the tragedian's art (*kata ten technen kalliste tragodia).* What he does is right (*orthon),* and therefore his success on the stage and in competitions is a very great sign (*semeion megiston).* Yet even the greatest sign is but a sign. Chapter 14 concludes by locating the objectively pitiful and fearsome in the action itself (*en tois pragmasin empoieteon)* by stating that the playwright should seek out (*tauta zeteteon)* actions (*pathe)* that occur or are about to occur among family members (*en tais philiais).*

The differentiation between the *mythos* as constitutively primary and the other five parts as constitutively secondary is necessary if the tragedy as a whole is to be a unity, not merely the sum of its parts. A tragedy is one not only because it is the imitation of one action (*holes praxeos)* but because it is structured around that one action (*peri mian praxin . . . synestesen;* 8.1451a28–29). As usual, Aristotle first establishes the unity of the formal-final cause and locates the actuality of the specific nature in it. The action as the direct object genitive of imitation (*mimesis praxeos)* in the formal definition is shown to be structurally a unity and emotively pitiful and fearsome and so tragic *(tragikon)*. Then, as usual, he shows how this action unifies and actualizes the other parts into a tragedy, which is more than the sum of its parts and has the holistic nature of the tragic. The other five parts, not being actually tragic in their own right, are potentially so, and that potentiality is actualized by the action as compositional principle. The shift from the direct object genitive "of the action" *(praxeos)* in chapter 6 to the compositional "around the action" *(peri praxin)* in chapter 8 marks the normal succession of two stages in an Aristotelian constitutive analysis. For unless the complex soul of a living animal is itself one, it cannot unify all the parts of its body into one animal. And unless it is the animal's specific nature as actuality, it cannot actualize the corresponding potentiality of all the parts of its body. As a fish must be one and specifically fishy in its entire being, so a tragedy must be one and specifically tragic in its entire being. And for that to be possible, its action must function analogously to the fish's soul *(arche men oun kai hoion psyche ho mythos tes tragodias;* 6.1450a38–39).

It can function in this way because the secondary parts are never independent of the compositional principle at all but are already chosen by the poet in the light of, and as suitable for, the latter. Chapter 17 sets out how the work of composition should proceed *(dei)*. The poet's basic work is to structure an action *(mythous synistanai):* "Whether the story exists already or whether he makes it himself, he should lay out the general structure" *(tous te logous kai tous pepoiemenous dei kai auton poiounta extithesthai katholou;* 17.1455a34–b1). The examples Aristotle gives of such general plot-structure *(theoreisthai to katholou)* show that emotive content is embedded in them, for they include not only the causal sequence of actions but also the family relationships that are constitutive of the pitiful and fearsome. Only after this structural-emotive core has been completed *(eith, meta)*, should the poet enlarge the tragedy by adding episodes and names. The names *(onomata)* would presumably carry *ethe* and *dianoia* with them, since these were not included in the general structure. The important compositional work is to make the episodes, and surely also the names with their associated characters and articulated rationality, integral *(oikeia)* to the general plot-structure. They should be of its household, selected in its light, and suitable to it. Such suitability consists partly in appropriate length, but *oikeia* is not merely a quantitative designation. Suitability is potentiality, which means that the secondary constitutive parts are chosen so as to make it possible for the action to unify them into one tragedy and to actualize them as tragic.

Some examples of how the compositional principle accomplishes this are given. Chapter 13 extends the notion of structure *(systasis)* and even of *mythos* to encompass both the action and the characters matched to it, and the suitability or potentiality of the characters is actualized as tragic only within this extended pattern. Chapter 9 briefly (9.1451b8–10) and chapter 15 in more detail (15.1454a33–36) extend the structural bonds of unity (necessity or probability) from the action to encompass the characters as well. The characters matched to the action must be suitable to it in the sense of being compatible with it, so that such speech or action pertains to them by probability or necessity (*toi poioi ta poia atta symbainei legein e prattein kata to eikos e to anankaion;* 9.1451b8–9). Chapter 15 licenses even wickedness *(ponerias)*, if it is artistically necessary (15.1454a28–29; cf. 25.1461b19–21). The language *(lexis)* must be appropriate *(oikeion, harmotton, prepon)*, as determined by the nature of tragedy itself (*aute he physis to oikeion metron heure;* 4.1449a24). Chapter 22 shows that such appropriateness lies partly in moderation in the use of its garnishings, but that it is also very precise since the change of a single word can destroy it (22.1458b11–9a16). Chapter 24 repeats that different meters are appropriate to different kinds of poetic works by their very nature *(aute he physis;* 24.1459b31–60a5) and concludes by showing how the ranking of *lexis* as fourth constitutive part governs its deployment *(diaponein)*, making it subsequent not only to the action but even to characters and to articulated rationality (24.1460b2–5). Chapter 18 demands that even the chorus and with it the fifth constitutive part *(melopoiia)* be integrated into the unity of the tragedy as a whole (18.1456a25–32).

To sum up this rather lengthy section: the action functions as compositional principle with a fine responsiveness to the distinct potentiality of each of the five secondary parts. Each part contributes a distinct dimension to the holistic tragic nature of the tragedy, which is actualized by the action around which they are structured. This provides good textual indications for the presence of immanent causal form-matter constitution in the category of *ousia*.

3.1.5 The Ontological and Cognitive Priority of the Object

The ontological and cognitive priority of the tragedy in itself *(auto kath hauto)* and in its own nature *(ten hautes physin)* is implied throughout. Aristotle safeguards it on two fronts, against the subjectivity of the playwright on the one hand and against that of a recipient on the other hand. It is notable that the language of the *Poetics* is objective and impersonal when it refers to the tragedy, and that most references to persons (playwrights, actors, producers, recipients) are pejorative. So far from taking empirical facts *(ta gignomena)* of a subjective nature as the norm by which a tragedy should be judged, Aristotle takes the objective nature of tragedy as the norm by which all subjective facts should be judged. What playwrights, actors, and producers do and what a recipient experiences may or may not be appropriate. The measure of appropriateness is the tragedy itself in its paradigm form: the tragedy that is finest according to the standard of the art (*he kata ten technen kalliste tragodia*; 13.1453a22–23). The norm and measure lies in the art itself, in the artistic *techne*, whose defining *telos* is its product. That product is the tragedy.

Subjective factors in the making or reception of a tragedy can fall short of this standard in two ways, through lack of understanding and through lack of integrity. Aristotle takes playwrights and recipients to task for both. Playwrights (with the exception of Homer and a few good tragedians) appear to him to be generally sadly lacking in understanding of their own craft, of the generic nature of art as imitation. They by and large do not comprehend that a poet is an imitator and that what he imitates is an action. They do not understand the compositional significance of this generic definition of art and so cannot be guided by the standard of the art, doing instead "what the playwright, but not the plot, requires" (*ha bouletai ho poietes all' ouch ho mythos*; 16.1454b34–35). This lack of understanding is widespread and is common also among recipients, who therefore cannot receive a tragedy appropriately and instead seek inappropriate pleasures in the theatre (cf. 1.1447b13–23; 8.1451a16–22; 16.1454b30–36; 23.1459a29–b2; 24.1460a5–9). But even if the standard of the *techne* is understood, lack of integrity may lead playwrights, actors, producers, and recipients not to honor it. The playwright may sell it out for the sake of indulging his own wilfulness, of pleasing actors and producers or audiences, producing what he wants or what they want rather than the finest tragedy. This may bring him acclaim from the many, but not from Aristotle, for whom *techne* and *technites* are terms of honor. Actors and producers may put their own desire for professional success ahead of the tragedy, using it rather than serving it. And recipients, though understanding the requirements of appropriate reception, may indulge their own weakness for happy endings, moralism, or cheap thrills (cf. 9.1451b33–2a1; 13.1453a33–36; 14.1453b7–11).

The common thread in Aristotle's numerous complaints is that subjective factors are made prior to the objective standard of the *techne*, which is grounded in the generic nature of art as imitation. Art is defined as imitation, its products are generically defined as having representational content. This sets art apart as a distinctive subject genus in its own right, as a distinctive *techne* with standards of rightness that are different from those of any other *techne*. Hence, the ontological and cognitive priority of artistic objects is generically grounded. For any and all subjective factors, whether on the producing or on the receiving side, themselves lack representational content. Making them prior is an error (*hamartanein*), because it contravenes the standards that pertain to artistic *techne* (*ta pros auten ten technen*), it is "a failure in imitation" (*amimetos*; 25.1460b32). A tragedy is ontologically and cognitively prior, not because it is tragic, but because it is a work of art. Chapter 25 sets out the nature of artistic *techne* as *mimesis* and uses it as the conceptual basis for solving *aporiai*. Neither a playwright nor a recipient can be a constitutive or definitory part of what a tragedy is in is own nature. That is why neither is listed as such a part in chapter 6. Both are posterior to the tragedy, since both are connected with it only by transeunt efficient causality, not by immanent formal-final or material constitutive causality.

To recapitulate: the first level, being *(panta ta onta)*, is present in the *Poetics* both in the sense that a tragedy is conceptualized as being and in the sense that Aristotle's distinctive understanding of being is brought to bear on it. The pervasive conceptual constants of which that distinctive understanding consists (the concept of being, the categories of being, the categorial priority of *ousia*, immanent causal form-matter constitution in the category of *ousia*, the ontological and cognitive priority of the object) are present in the *Poetics*.

3.2 The Second and Third Levels: Mimesis 1 and Mimesis 2

The general notion of craft is not directly present in the text of the *Poetics*, but there are enough indirect textual indications to make its presence clear. The word *techne* itself appears frequently, though usually in the more restricted sense of artistic *techne*. However, the more restricted sense implies the more general, since art as a subdivision of craft is itself a craft (see Section 2.4 above). A tragedy has to be understood as a product of *techne*.

That means that in its own being it relates to the products of nature in terms of structural or constitutive imitation (*mimesis* 1), which is the basis of analogy. Aristotle explicitly relates a tragedy to a living animal *(zoon)* by analogy, and at 21.1457b16–18 he defines analogy as structural or constitutive similarity (A:B = C:D), so that there is no doubt that he understands it in the *Poetics* in the same way as in the *Metaphysics* and elsewhere. It follows that his use of analogy has the same implications as elsewhere.

The most important of the tragedy-animal analogies occurs in chapter 6, just after Aristotle ends the definitional account and begins the functional account at 6.1450a15. He begins it by immediately singling the action (the *mythos* or *systasis pragmaton*) out as the most important *(megiston)* of the six constitutive parts, and the reason he gives anticipates the argument of chapter 8 that life is focused on an individual person *(peri hena)* but art on an individual action *(peri mian praxin)*. The action functions as the tragedy's compositional principle, which Aristotle expresses by calling it the tragedy's final cause *(telos)* and *arche*.

The tragedy-animal analogy occurs in this context, actually in the same sentence in which Aristotle designates the action as the tragedy's *arche*. He likens the tragedy's action to an animal's soul, which means that they function similarly in the intrinsic being of the entities whose *archai* they are: A:B = C:D. The action of a tragedy is to the other five constitutive parts as the soul of an animal is to its body. Both function as immanent formal-final cause, as *arche*. *Mimesis* 1 is clearly implied in its normal meaning and technical precision. A tragedy imitates in its own being the inner form-matter (actuality-potentiality) constitution of a living animal.

Commentators have noted this and have noted that the analogy must be taken very seriously and understood in its normal Aristotelian sense. Yet they have been reluctant to draw its normal Aristotelian implications, e.g., to let a tragedy's action function analogously to a living creature's soul. This is the more puzzling as the analogy occurs in the definitional chapter (chapter 6) in the context of Aristotle's functional account, which singles the action out as constitutive formal-final cause and *arche*.[26] One reason for this reluctance may be a point noted above (see Section 3.1.3), namely, that commentators have focused on the content of Aristotle's formal definition of tragedy and have not considered the status and implications of such a definition. One implication is that Aristotle's terminology in such a context is technical, not colloquial. *Telos* is final cause for him, not purpose or goal or end or any other of the less technical terms by which *telos* tends to be translated. And *arche* is in the singular in the text, as are *telos* and *ergon*, which means that the action is the only definitory final cause. The singulars are incompatible with some commentators' preference for multiple *tele*.[27] Another reason for the commentators' reluctance may be that the analogy designates a tragedy as an *ousia*, for only an *ousia* has its own immanent governing *arche*. Accidents have the *ousia* in which they inhere as their governing *arche* (cf. *Met.* VII.1). A tragedy imitates the constitutively self-governing and hence independent and separate being of a living animal, for its action "besouls" it, just as the soul does the animal. Accepting the categorization of works of art as *ousiai* means understanding them from a cosmo-centric perspective *(techne* imitates *physis)*, something that commentators are reluctant to do due to their strong anthropocentric orientation, particularly in theory of art. One final reason for their reluctance may be Halliwell's comment, already cited (see Section 3.1 above), that modern readers are inevitably out of sympathy with Aristotle's text. Part of that lack of sympathy may lie in our different habit of thinking. We tend to think more laterally and cumulatively, particularly in theory of art, finding Aristotle's definitional, paradigmatic, and technical thinking uncongenial. Whatever the reasons, understanding the analogy in Aristotle's sense entails drawing its Aristotelian implications.

The analogies between a tragedy and a living animal in chapters 7 (7.1450b34–36) and 23 (23.1459a17–21) are less important than the one in chapter 6. But the one in chapter 23 is significant in drawing an Aristotelian implication of the analogy: like an animal, a tragedy is self-constituting as one whole *(hen holon)* prior to any efficiently causal effect *(poie)* it may have on any other *ousia*. For an animal and a tragedy produce such transeunt effects in the secondary category of doing *(poiein)* only as what they are in their own substantial being, since *poiein*, too, is *pros hen* focused on them as *ousiai*. The pleasure a tragedy produces in a recipient is therefore subsequent to it *(apo tes tragodias;* 13.1453a35–36), and so appropriate to it *(oikeia)*. It cannot be prior to it in the sense of being constitutive or definitory of its being, any more than the aesthetic pleasure derived from contemplating an animal can be constitutive of the animal's own being. Aristotle's recipients achieve appropriate reception only if they understand and are affected by a work of art as a whole, not piecemeal, and if they receive it as what it is in its own right. The same is true of epic:

> As for the narrative art in spoken verse, it is obvious that as in tragedies, it should compose its plot-structures dramatically and around a single action which is whole and complete . . . so that like an animal which is one and a whole it produces *(poiei)* its appropriate pleasure. (23.1459a17–21)

The second level, craft *(techne)* and *mimesis* 1, is present in the *Poetics* in these analogies. It is worth noting that the natural paradigm that a tragedy imitates in its inner constitution is Aristotle's strongest and clearest sublunary *ousia*, a living animal, whose own being has the strongest potentiality-actuality unity and integration.

There is direct evidence that the third level is present in the text, since *mimesis* 2 is the definitory generic nature of all works of art. There is also direct evidence that levels 4 and 5, verbal and tragic artistic *techne*, are present.

To sum up this section: the levels of the schema that sketches the location of a tragedy within Aristotle's conceptual space (see Section 2.4 above) and within which the being of a tragedy must therefore be understood *ex Aristotele*, are either directly or indirectly present in the text of the *Poetics*. There is no textual indication that any one of them is not present or not relevant. What emerges is a picture of the *Poetics* as a treatise with a distinctive subject matter of its own, with standards and norms of excellence of its own, which Aristotle understands in terms of his normal conceptual framework. In fact, he deliberately brings that framework to bear on the resolution of *aporiai* in chapter 25.

One consequence of this result is that Aristotle's terminology is much more technical and *pros hen* focused than that of his commentators. Another consequence is that the preference of commentators for understanding the essential being of a tragedy as both *auto-telic* and *hetero-telic* is incompatible with Aristotle's distinctive understanding of being, as it is present in the *Poetics*. Nothing can be definitorily both *auto-telic* and *hetero-telic* for him, nothing can be essentially defined both in the categories of *ousia* and of *pros ti*. The categories allow him to understand the being of a tragedy in both categories, but in strict *pros hen* priority of *ousia*. *Kath hauto* and *pros allo* are not co-ordinate, instead the latter is subordinate to the former. "And what is relative *(pros ti)* is least of all a definite nature *(physis tis)* and *ousia,* and is posterior to the qualitative and the quantitative" (*Met.* XIV. 1088a22–24; cf. *E.N.* I. 6. 1096a20–22). Appreciating the technical precision of Aristotle's terminology and the presence of his distinctive understanding of being in the *Poetics* saves one from imputing to him the (in his view) worst possible category mistake.[28]

3.3 The Aporia of Mimesis and Aristotle's Solution

But the presence of all the levels of the schema in the *Poetics* does not save Aristotle from an *aporia*, which arises on his own terms, *ex Aristotele*. He does not acknowledge this *aporia*, yet it emerges as the central conceptual problem in his theory of art. It is the relationship of *mimesis* 1 and *mimesis* 2. For a tragedy must imitate nature both structurally-constitutively and representationally, it must imitate both the inner constitution and *ousia*-hood of a living animal and the descriptive content of human life.

This would not be a conceptual problem if the two kinds of imitation were simply additive. But they are not. *Mimesis* 1, as the more general, is presupposed by and authoritative for *mimesis* 2. A tragedy must therefore imitate (1) a living animal's inner constitution, by imitating (2) the descriptive content of human life, it must achieve *mimesis* 1 by means of *mimesis* 2. Yet *mimesis* 2 is its definitory generic nature, which as a distinct subject genus must have a distinct descriptive content.

The problem can be formulated in a variety of ways: how can what has representational content as its definitory generic nature be isomorphic in constitutive structure with something that does not? How can what imitates (2) the descriptive content of another *ousia* be an *ousia* in its own right with a generically and specifically new and distinct descriptive content? How can a copy be an original? How can a representational work of art be simultaneously *of* a recognizable extra-artistic object and yet a work of art in its own right? How can it be self-referential, self-significant, and self-worthy in its own being by being other-related in its representational content? How can an artist be an imitator in his generic definition *(mimetes)* and yet a maker *(poietes)?* Yet the formula *poietes mimetes* pervades the *Poetics* as a foundational conceptualization. The problem is unavoidable because it pertains to all representational art, and it centers on the inconspicuous two-letter word *of*. It was earlier alluded to as the quarrel between Plato and Aristotle concerning the ontological status of works of art (see Section 2.2 above), and that quarrel recurs now from within the Aristotelian framework itself. But even though he does not acknowledge it as an *aporia*, he resolves it in a way that anticipates Kandinsky's resolution early in our century (see *Conclusion* below).[29] For Aristotle, a representational work of art is possible by means of the interplay of three ways in which the artist (or rather art itself as an impersonal *techne*) relates to his objects of imitation *(mimesis* 2): there are liberties he may not take with them, there are liberties he may take with them, there are liberties he must take with them. The first preserves a recognizable representational content, the second gives a range of options, the third transforms a copy into an original, a painted *bed* into a *painting* of a bed, *mimesis* 2 into a way of achieving *mimesis* 1.

3.3.1 Liberties Art May Not Take

It is clear that there are liberties that art may not take with the objects it imitates, which form its representational content. For license in this regard would destroy the representational content and so the generic definition and thereby art itself as a distinctive subject genus. Liberties art may not take thus safeguard the basic relationship between art and life as *mimesis* 2 and provide the framework within which art may and must take liberties.

Art may not take into its own representational content objects that have no reality in life at all. That reality may be factual (past or present fact; *hoia en e estin;* 25.1460b8–11; *genomena;* 9.1451b29–32). It may be probable *(eikos)* in the sense of generally *(katholou)* being in character *(toi poioi ta poia;* 9.1451b5–11). It may be mythical (the traditional stories, *tous te logous kai tous pepoiemenous;* 17.1455a34–b1). It may be ethical (what should be according to ethical standards, *hoia einai dei;* 25.1460b8–11; 25.1460b33–35). It may be opinion (what people say, *hoia phasin kai dokei;* 25.1460b8–11; 25.1460b33–35). The artist may and must change and even invent *(auton poiounta;* 17.1455a34–b1) within but not beyond these parameters, which suffice to give a work of art a representational content that bears some recognizable similarity to life. In this wide and flexible Aristotelian sense, art is realistic. *Poietes* refers to what he may and must do within these parameters, *mimetes* refers to the parameters themselves.

Art may not reject all the constraints life exerts on the descriptive content of the objects it imitates. These are both logical and ethical. For example, because actions imply agents, who in turn imply character and articulated rationality, a tragedy, defined as the imitation of an action *(mimesis praxeos)*, has *mythos*, ethe, and *dianoia* as three distinct constitutive parts falling under the differentia objects of imitation *(ha)*. The necessity *(ananke)*, the logical force of these implications, obtains in art as in life and sets the parameters within which art can use *ethe* and *dianoia* (e.g., 2.1448a1–5; 6.1449b36–50a5). The ethical constraints are real and objective for Aristotle and relevant in art as in life, since art may not contravene them except by artistic necessity (25.1461b19–21; 15.1454a28–29). In terms of such logical and ethical constraints, art is more deeply similar to life than in terms of mere facts.

Art may not make a factual mistake with regard to life *(ouk alethe; hamartia)* or contravene life's logical and ethical standards gratuitously, without artistic necessity. Any departure from recognizable similarity to life must be required by the intrinsic standards of rightness *(orthotes)* of art. Only these standards can override the need for similarity. They are generically grounded *(poietes mimetes; hos kata ten mimesin poietas; 1.1447b14–15; 9.1451b27–29; 25.1460b8–11)*, and so they safeguard the similarity to life while establishing the generic distance between life and art. Art is as similar to life in descriptive content as it is possible for it as a distinctive subject genus to be (25.1460b13–35; 25.1461b19–21).

Art may not relegate the objects it imitates to a marginal role in its own inner being but must give them definitory generic and specific significance. For *mimesis* 2 is its generic nature, and the objects of imitation are one type of differentia *(ha)* and so enter into the specific definitions of the several species of art. These species are generically the same in terms of *mimesis* 2 but specifically different in terms of differences among these objects *(hetera, 1.1447a16–18; 2.1448a16–18)*. The similarity to life is both generic and specific.

Art may not avoid similarity to life by conceptualizing a work of art as a *logos*, as the poet's direct or indirect speaking. This would remove works of art from the object-level and put them on the metalevel of *logoi*, which are about *(peri)* beings *(onta)*, but are not themselves *onta*. *Mimesis* 2 is a relationship between two *onta*, while *logoi* relate to *onta* by correspondence. This is why *logoi* can be true or false, but *onta* cannot. Therefore the verses of Empedocles are *logoi*, not *mimeseis* (1.1447b13–24), even though ancient Greek poets and ordinary people, as well as past and present commentators tend to make this mistake. Homer, as usual, knew better: "Among Homer's many other laudable attributes is his grasp—unique among poets—of his status as poet. For the poet himself should speak as little as possible, since when he does so he is not engaging in *mimesis*" (24.1460a5–8). The poet, to use Else's memorable phrase, lurks neither behind nor in his characters (see chapter 2, Note 8).

3.3.2 Liberties Art May Take

There are actually very few liberties art may take. The text gives a deceptive appearance of choices, which is due to Aristotle's speaking on the generic level. Generically, the characters to be imitated are either good or bad or like ourselves (e.g., 2.1448a1–5; cf. chapter 13). But specifically they are determined by the nature (*physis*) of each species of art. So comedy imitates inferior characters, epic and tragedy superior ones (e.g., 2.1448a16–18; 5.1449a32–33; 5.1449b9–10). As usual, generic possibilities are specifically actualized and determined.

The only two genuine liberties seem to lie in a poet's choice between using traditional stories, changing them, or making up new ones (9.1451b19–25; 17.1455a34–b1) and between preserving similarity to life through imitating objects as they were or are, as they are said to be, or as they ought to be (25.1460b8–11). The first range of options indicates an indifference to the traditional myths on Aristotle's part, which contrasts rather sharply with our modern reverence. He characterizes excessive faithfulness as ridiculous (*geloion;* 9.1451b19–25).[30] The second range of options is not quite so clear-cut as it seems. For factual similarity (*ta genomena*, things as they were or are) is ambiguous. If it means that the objects art imitates must be found in life (actions, characters, articulated rationality are all found in human life), it is harmless enough. But if it means that they must be imitated *as* they are found in life, the distinctiveness of art as a subject genus would be destroyed and *mimesis* 2 would degenerate into mere copying, which in terms of descriptive content would no longer be artistic making (*poiesis*). Aristotle contrasts both life and history with art, because the three structure the same facts and factors differently: life structures them around a single human being (*peri hena*), history around a single time period (*peri hena chronon*), art around a single action (*peri mian praxin*). These different structures require differences in descriptive content (this will be argued presently). Aristotle is ill at ease with factual similarity, arguing that a poet is still a poet even if he imitates *genomena*, since nothing prevents some (*enia*) facts in life from arising according to probability (*eikos*), as they do in art (9.1451b29–32; but cf. 9.1451a36–38 and 9.1451b5–11). This is the only time he argues in this vein, but his insistence that the poet must above all make (*poiein*) the plot-structure implies that it is art-specific and not found in life. For a structure of events found in life need only be imitated as a whole or cut out of environing facts, it need not be made. I shall argue presently that the plot-structure of a tragedy is not only different from but incompatible with *praxis* as it occurs in life.

The reason for Aristotle's indifference to the traditional myths and for his unease with factual similarity of art to life is the same: art must construct its works according to artistic standards of rightness and may not brook interference from any others. The myths and life contain too much that is incompatible with artistic standards, and liberties may be taken in order to guard the integrity of those standards. Their austerity reflects not only Aristotle's fourth-century Greek Enlightenment rationality but also the clear recognition that only one standard can be authoritative, if a work of art is to be an integral whole with a distinctive nature of its own. Fidelity to art overrides fidelity to myth and to life. Aristotle would have had no more patience with "artistic licence" than with any other, since the excellence of artistic products depends on obedience to the objective standards of art.

3.3.3 Liberties Art Must Take

Liberties art must take are much more numerous and important than those it may take. The "must" is clearly expressed in the prescriptive force of words such as "necessity" (*ananke*), "ought" (*dei*), "must" (*chre*), which are remarkably numerous in the text, as well as in imperatives. It is equally clearly expressed by Aristotle's references to the intrinsic standards of rightness (*orthotes*) of artistic *techne* (chapter 25), to the paradigm of "the finest tragedy according to the standard of the *techne*" (*he men oun kata ten technen kalliste tragodia*; 13.1453a22–23), and to the poet's work (*poietou ergon*; 9.1451a36–38).

The "must" is grounded exclusively in the fidelity to art mentioned above, which not only may but must override fidelity to life. The objects of imitation must be transferred from one subject genus (life) to another (art), and transference across a generic dividing line requires transformation both functionally and in descriptive content. *An. Post.* elucidates the depth of generic differences by arguing that even the common axioms of demonstrative science are analogically, not identically, the same in different subject genera (see Introduction above). It is this depth that establishes subject genera as independent domains of being, each integral in its own right. An action as it occurs in life cannot be identical with an action as it occurs in art. The central question is to what extent and in what sense it can even be similar.

Commentators have recognized that imitation does not mean copying, that a tragedy's representational content is not identical with life. But they have perhaps not always appreciated the depth of the generic divide between art and life. For some hold that art takes forms from life and puts them into a new alien material or medium.[31] But this takes no cognizance of Aristotle's position that form and matter are correlative co-constitutive *archai* and not alien to one another, that a tragedy has integral holistic being rather than the external agonistic imposition of form on an alien matter, and that art's own intrinsic standard of rightness governs how it imitates life. Aspects of life enter the domain of art only on art's own terms.[32]

Something found in life (actions, characters, articulated rationality) is not merely transferred from one material to another, but from one *ousia* to another. It is taken out of its former context and re-contextualized. No aspect of its former function and descriptive content can remain unchanged, since any *ousia* is integrally and holistically *pros hen* focused on its own essential nature. Actions, characters, and articulated rationality function humanly in life—they function artistically in art. They each make a distinctive contribution to a human being in life—they each make a distinctive contribution to a work of art in art. Their descriptive content must be compatible with their function in life—it must be compatible with their function in art. Fundamentally different functions are not compatible with identical descriptive contents.

The functional differences between actions, characters, and articulated rationality in art and in life are spelled out in chapters 6 and 7, but they are argued for only in chapter 8. Action is singled out functionally, and this singling out is the foundational liberty art must take with its objects of imitation. For in life, action is in one of the secondary categories, and it is the agent who is singled out as *ousia* and *pros hen* focus. The formal definition of tragedy singles action out by listing it as the only immediate object of imitation *(estin oun tragodia mimesis praxeos)*. In the following analysis of this definition, characters *(ethe)* and articulated rationality *(dianoia)* are recognized as constitutive parts under the differentia objects of imitation *(ha)*, only because they are implied by action, not independently and in their own right. This is confirmed by the singling out of action as functionally or constitutively primary *(megiston, proton, telos, arche hoion psyche)*, while *ethe* and *dianoia* are secondary. Chapter 8 gives the reason for this singling out by contrasting life and art in terms of each one's vital center, around which the whole must be structured *(synistanai)*. Life is structured around one person *(peri hena)*, art around one action *(peri mian praxin)*. A person's vital center is the human soul, which as formal-final cause besouls all aspects of his being in *pros hen* focused unity. A tragedy's vital center is the action, which as formal-final cause "besouls" all aspects of its being in *pros hen* focused unity. Life is categorially and constitutively focused on an agent, art on an action.

The reason for this categorial and constitutive re-focusing is that the agent-focused structure of life cannot be imitated by art: it is natural, not artistic. It is found, not made. It does not have the art-specific nature of the tragic. A tragedy would be an imitation man in Plato's pejorative sense, if art did not re-focus its representational content, if a work of art did not have a vital center distinctively its own. The poet is a maker *(poietes)* foundationally by making *(poiein)* the action function as compositional principle, analogously to the soul of a living animal. It is the functional or constitutive re-focusing that marks the depth of the generic divide between life and art. All who disregard this foundational law of artistic composition are in error *(hamartanein;* chapter 8). An action must function differently in art than in life.

The human soul as the vital center of a human life gives distinctively human unity to all aspects of that life—but it could not give distinctively tragic unity to all aspects of a tragedy. For its functional role depends on its having the appropriate descriptive content. That descriptive content has two aspects, one structural and the other qualitative. The former is the soul's unity, while the latter is the specific nature of the human *(dipoun zoon)*. All souls in the genus animal have the structural aspect in common (since each must be a unity), but they differ qualitatively. Together, the two aspects give the human soul the appropriate descriptive content, which enables it to function as *eidos-telos* of a human life.

Analogously, the action as the vital center of a tragedy gives distinctively tragic unity to all aspects of that work of art—but it could not give distinctively human unity to all aspects of a human life. For its functional role depends on its having the appropriate descriptive content. That descriptive content has two aspects, one structural and the other qualitative. The former is the action's unity, while the latter is its specific qualitative nature of the tragic. All "souls" in the genus art have the structural aspect in common (since each must be a unity), but they differ qualitatively. Together, the two aspects give the action the appropriate descriptive content, which enables it to function as *eidos-telos* of a tragedy.

The action's functional role is the pervasive premise from which its descriptive content is derived. *Tragodia mimesis praxeos* in the formal definition singles the action out functionally as the object of imitation, whose descriptive content as specifically tragic (structurally and emotively) is said to be the tragedy's achievement *(perainousa)*. Chapter 7 derives the action's distinctive structural unity and wholeness from its functional priority (7.1450b21–23). Chapter 8 derives its structural unity and wholeness from its functional role of giving unity to the tragedy (making the tragedy a single *mimesis;* 8.1451a30–34). Chapters 9 and 11 link its emotive content with its structure (9.1452a1–4; 11.1452a36–b3). The art-specific structural unity and emotive content together give the action the appropriate descriptive content, the specific nature of the tragic, which enables it to "besoul" a tragedy as a whole. For what makes pitiful and fearsome events tragic is their incorporation in the action's structure. When they occur in life outside this structure, they are not tragic.

The liberties art must take with its objects of imitation arise from the need to make *mimesis* 2 serve *mimesis* 1, so that a tragedy can be an artistic *ousia* governed by artistic lawfulness, analogous to a natural *ousia* governed by natural lawfulness. This is achieved in an art-specific way by severe selectiveness and by re-focusing. The selectiveness consists in taking but three aspects of life as objects of imitation *(praxis, ethe, dianoia)*, which conspicuously leaves the human being himself out.[33] It further involves singling one of these three out as functionally primary and so as the primary locus of the specifically tragic *(to tragikon)*. It is not the representational content as such *(praxis, ethe, dianoia)* that serves as compositional principle, but only one part of it, the action. And even of this, only *mythos*, i.e., the structural aspect which incorporates the emotive content, is singled out.

The resolution of Aristotle's central *aporia* is successful but comes at a price. Halliwell has noted that *mimesis* 2 is not too close to copying but rather not close enough, that recognizable similarity with life wears thin. In order to strengthen it, he goes so far as to oppose a crucial bracketing, not on textual but on exegetical grounds.[34] He faults Aristotle for conjoining necessity and probability in the structural unity of the action, since few if any things in life happen by necessity. But if the above account has merit, Aristotle may indeed have conjoined them because the unity of the action is not lifelike but art-specific. It may be their distance from life, rather than their closeness to it which commends them. For this unity is the principle of art, in terms of which the action unifies the whole tragedy and so "besouls" it.[35] But if so, Halliwell has seen a serious problem with Aristotle's solution of his *aporia:* is the price he has to pay too high? Just how thin can recognizable similarity wear, before it loses any significant sense and before *mimesis* 2 ceases to function as the definitory generic nature of art? The action in a tragedy is unlike any action found in life both functionally and in descriptive content. Chapter 4 will pursue this problem by presenting a comparison between the constitutive structure of a tragedy in the *Poetics,* that of ethical human life in the *Nichomachean Ethics,* and that of rhetorical speechmaking in the *Rhetoric.*

Chapter 4

AGENT-CENTERING, PATIENT-CENTERING, OBJECT-CENTERING

The central *aporia*, which arises for Aristotle's theory of art *ex Aristotele* has so far been elucidated from the *Poetics*, and Halliwell has diagnosed its main danger: *mimesis* 2 may wear too thin to bear the generic definitory burden which Aristotle places on it. The parameters set by the liberties art may not take with its objects of imitation may not suffice to contain the liberties that it may and must take within a recognizable similarity between art and life.

That danger appears even greater when one elucidates the *aporia* not only from the text of the *Poetics* but comparatively from the text of the *Nicomachean Ethics* as well. Tragic and ethical action, *praxis* in a tragedy *(Poetics)* and *praxis* in a human life *(E.N.)*, appear not only different but mutually incompatible. The comparison will provide the basis for a more adequate assessment of Aristotle's ability to resolve his central *aporia*. It will also clarify to what extent the *Poetics* should be read in the light of the *E.N.* This will provide the basis for polemical engagement: to what extent does a tragedy have didactic significance as a mirror of life? What, if anything, can it teach us about life? Since the mirror-of-life didactic exegesis is still prevalent, the comparison will provide data in terms of which its validity can be assessed.[1]

A second comparison, between the *Poetics* and the *Rhetoric*, will be added entirely for polemical reasons. For unlike the essential definitory link between art and life (*mimesis* 2), there is no essential link between

Poetics and *Rhetoric*. Nor does the question of how art relates to rhetoric arise out of Aristotle's central *aporia,* and so it does not impinge on the success or failure of his theory of art. Art and rhetoric are neither in the same subject genus, nor is rhetoric generically defined as imitation (*mimesis* 2), nor is art generically defined as imitation (*mimesis* 2) of rhetoric. Yet commentators have read the *Poetics* in the light of the *Rhetoric,* and a comparison of tragic and rhetorical action, *praxis* in the *Poetics* and *praxis* in the *Rhetoric,* will provide the basis for a clarification of the relationship of the two texts.[2]

The two comparisons have a common focus on action, for it is the functional role and descriptive content of *praxis* in the three texts that will be compared. The crucial question is the relationship of *praxis* with *ousia* in each text. For whether *praxis* is an attribute in a secondary category *(poiein or pros ti)* or a causally constitutive first principle *(arche)* in the primary category of *ousia,* it must be related to an individual entitative *ousia,* since Aristotelian metaphysics allows neither accidents nor *archai* to be separately and independently. Accidents are posterior to *ousiai* while *archai* are constitutively prior to them, but in neither case could a *praxis* be on its own. Ethical action, rhetorical action, tragic action each need to be linked with an individual *ousia.* There are only three possible *ousiai* with which actions can be linked: an agent, a patient, an object. Ethical action is agent-centered on the ethical agent, rhetorical action (speechmaking) is patient-centered on the audience, and tragic action is object-centered on the tragedy. Hence the title of this chapter.

4.1 Agent-Centering and Object-Centering (Ethical and Tragic Action)

4.1.1 Agent-Centering (Ethical Action)[3]

Ethical action *(spoudaiai energeiai, hai kat' areten praxeis, eupraxia)* is an attribute of a human agent (who is the *ousia*) in the secondary category of doing *(poiein).* Its functional role, like that of all other actions in life, is to be an active goal-directed dimension of human living. Hence, the *Nicomachean Ethics* starts: "Every craft and every inquiry, and similarly every action and pursuit, is thought to aim at some good" (*E.N.* I.1.1094 a 1–2). The role of actions is to attain some good or *telos* of the human agent, clearly a *pros hen* dependent function. Actions differ because the goods or *tele* which the agent wishes to obtain differ. And their *tele* are the definitory principles of actions *(hai men gar archai ton prakton to hou heneka ta prakta; E.N.* VI.5.1140b16–17; cf. VII.8.1151a15–16).

The good or *telos* of ethical actions differs from that of all other actions. It is the living out of ethical goodness, since the agent acts "for the sake of the noble" *(tou kalou heneka; E.N.* IV.1.1120a24). This *telos* is most fundamentally different from that of actions that are makings or productions *(poieseis)*, whose *telos* is a product different from and beyond *(heteron kai para)* the activity of making. Hence the *Nicomachean Ethics*, having started by declaring that every action aims at some good, immediately differentiates those goods or *tele:* "But a certain difference is found among ends; some are activities *(energeiai)*, others are products *(erga)* beyond the activities" *(E.N.* I.1.1094a3–5). Ethical actions, unlike all makings or productions, have no extrinsic product as their *telos,* and hence ethical living is not a *techne (E.N.* VI.4,5).

Less fundamentally, ethical actions are also differentiated from actions that are motions *(kinesis, genesis)* which, even if not making a product, have an extrinsic *telos* in the sense of a limit *(E.N.* X.4.1174a19–b5). And they are differentiated from actions that, while neither makings nor motions, are not ethical. Among these Aristotle usually lists seeing, thinking, understanding, enjoying (e.g., *Met.* IX.6; *E.N.* X.4,3). Ethical actions are living well and being happy *(eu zen, eu prattein, eudaimonia, euzoïa, eupraxia; E.N.* I.8.1098b20–22; 13.1102a5–6). Linguistically they are marked by the adverb "well" *(eu;* or other adverbs).

The distinctive functional role of ethical actions is agent-centered in a distinctive way. Generally, all actions in life are the acting of a human agent, directed to his goals or *tele* and initiated and terminated by him. The human agent is the *arche* of all his actions *(anthropos einai arche ton praxeon; E.N.* III.3.1112b31–32). But ethical actions are agent-centered in a uniquely intimate manner. For unlike all productions and motions, the agent himself is their defining *telos,* so that agent-centering consists in the coincidence of initiating *(hothen)* and final *(hou heneka)* cause, of *arche* in both of these senses. And unlike other actions whose final cause is intrinsic to them (e.g., seeing, thinking, understanding, enjoying), ethical actions have as their defining *telos* the agent's own human good *(ton anthropinon agathon)* and happiness: "[H]uman good turns out to be activity of soul in accordance with excellence" *(E.N.* I.7.1098a16–17), "for we have practically defined happiness as living well and acting well" *(E.N.* I.8.1098b20–21). Since ethical actions involve both ethical and intellectual excellence *(aretas ethous, aretas dianoias),* the human good which is their defining *telos* is complete in the sense of being cognitively correct, ethically best, emotively happy and pleasant, as gauged by the practically wise man *(ho phronimos, ho spoudaios)* who is the objective norm and measure *(kanon kai metron; E.N.* II.6.1106b36–7a2; III.4.1113a31–33; VI.5.1140a24–28; X.5.1176a15–19; X.6.1176b24–26). Ethical actions are agent-centered, not empirically on the agent as he is, but normatively on the agent as he ought to be at his human best: "Since happiness is an activity of soul in accordance with complete excellence" *(kat' areten teleian; E.N.* I.13.1102a5–6).

The descriptive content of ethical actions is commensurate with this functional role both structurally and qualitatively *(poion)*. Structurally, ethical actions are determined by their categorial status as attributes of a human agent in the secondary category of doing *(poiein)*. Agent-centering means structurally that such actions not only originate from the agent but also have accordance with his ethical character as their defining *telos* *(telos de pases energeias esti to kata ten hexin; E.N. III.7.1115b20–21)*. Using a spatial metaphor, one could describe their structure as circular, as finite and determinate acts of living whose origin and defining *telos* coincide in a single *ousia*, the agent. Hence, they do not fall into the category of the relative *(pros ti)*, whose origin and defining *telos* diverge, since for Aristotle a relation holds between two different *ousiai*. Anything falling into the category of *pros ti* can therefore be represented by the spatial metaphor of a straight line. To anticipate the second half of this chapter: the circular line represents agent-centering, the straight one patient-centering.

It follows that ethical actions are never means to any extrinsic end *(pros ti, allou charin, chresimon, di' allo haireton, allou heneka, heteron to telos, todi dia todi)*. Nor do they have an extrinsic *telos* in the sense of a limit. Hence, they are structurally unlike all such actions: they have no parts *(mere)* different from the whole action and from each other in form *(eidei)*, they are not internally temporally successive *(ephexes)*, they have no internal links of efficient causality *(dia)*, they are never incomplete but complete in their form *(eidei)* at every moment (cf. *E.N.* X.4). Hence, they are loved and valued for themselves *(kath hauta; E.N. I.5.1096b3–6)*.[4]

Their qualitative nature as ethical *(ethike)* is vividly agent-centered to such an extent that they are properly characterized as ethically good only adverbially *(eu)*, not adjectivally *(agathe)*. As usual, the grammatical form reflects a mode of being. Adjectival being is those *pros hen* focused properties that characterize an *ousia* (cf. *Met.* IX.7) and in terms of which it is said to be such-and-such *(E.N. IV.3.1123a35–b1)*. Adverbial being is not properties of an action itself but the way the agent carries it out *(E.N. II.4.1105a26–33)*. Actions are not ethically good *(agathe)* but done in an ethically good manner *(eu)*. An action, taken on its own, is not ethically good except accidentally *(kata symbebekos; E.N. V.9.1136a25–28; V.9.1137a21–23)*. An agent is ethically good *(agathos)* and therefore does an action ethically well *(eu)*. The ethical nature of an action is entirely derivative from the agent, its adverbial being from his adjectival being. Man's ethical living is uniquely agent-centered because the ethical nature of an action is not determined by anything extrinsic to the agent himself.

But ethical agent-centering is neither empirical nor subjective or relative, but normative. For an agent acts ethically well only if he does an action as it should be done, according to the practically wise man as objective norm and measure: "For practical wisdom issues commands, since its end is what should be done or not" (*he men gar phronesis epitaktike estin; ti gar dei prattein e me, to telos autes estin; E.N.* VI.10.1143a8–9). A given individual acts ethically well only if "he acts as just and temperate men act" (*alla kai houto pratton hos hoi dikaioi kai sophrones prattousin; E.N.* II.4.1105b5–9).

Ethical agent-centering is multidimensional, and its four dimensions (causal, volitional, cognitive, moral) are ways of exerting control (*kyria, arche*). An action is ethically well done only if the agent (*ho pratton*) has control over his action (*to prattomenon*) in each of these four ways. If one or more are weak or ineffective (as, e.g., in *akrasia*), the agent still does the action but does not do it ethically well (*eu*).

Causal control consists in the action's being in the agent's own power and so voluntary: "[T]he voluntary would seem to be that of which the principle lies in the agent himself" (*to hekousion doxeien an einai hou he arche en autoi; E.N.* III.1.1111a22–23). Book III differentiates being in one's own power (*eph hemin, en hemin*) from not being so, such as: an action that is not possible (*dynaton*) in the sense that it cannot be done (*prakton*) or brought about by our own effort (*di' hemon genoit' an*); an action that depends on anything fortuitous (*tychei*); an action that is caused by factors external to the agent (*aitia en tois ektos, exothen he arche, para tes en hemin*) such as compulsion (*bia*) and ignorance (*agnoia*).

Causal control is exerted by the agent over actions that are humanly possible and doable, not fortuitous, independent of external factors, and not caused by either compulsion or ignorance. Aristotle holds the agent to the practically wise man's standard of what is humanly possible by holding him responsible for his own ethical character and cognitive ability to know what is actually good and not only seems so. He marginalizes fate and chance and all that is external to the agent, pushing them to the periphery of ethical living as mere additions (*prosdeitai*) which do not affect the ethical quality of actions (*to eu e kakos*) or happiness (*E.N.* I.10). And he holds that force or ignorance exculpate the agent (unless he bears some contributory responsibility for them). The emphasis on causal control not only places ethical causality and accountability within the agent, but makes him nearly immune to any external factors. Agent-centering in this dimension means that an action, to be ethically well done, must be clearly and solely the agent's own action.

Volitional control consists in the action's being desired by the agent for its own sake and with deliberate choice. Aristotle's central volitional term is *orexis,* desire or stretching out toward something in a wide sense, which is narrowed down to a precise ethical sense. The first narrowing down consists in making all desire or stretching out *telic,* so that it is directed at something, rather than being random or blind. The second consists in making it rational (in Plato's and Aristotle's sense) by identifying its *telos* with a good *(agathou tinos)*. The third consists in making this good intrinsic and final rather than a means to some further end *(he gar eupraxia telos, he d'orexis toutou;* VI.2.1139a35–b4; cf. VI.5.1140b4–7; X.6.1176b6–9). The fourth consists in identifying it with ethical excellence *(tou kalou heneka;* E.N. IV.1.1120a23–24).

And the fifth consists in making ethical excellence the object of deliberate choice *(prohairesis),* which involves understanding its objective value as the human good and happiness (e.g., *E.N.* I.7.1098a16–18) and consciously preferring it to other lesser goods *(pro heteron haireton;* E.N. III.2.1112a15–17).

Agent-centering in this dimension means that the agent makes the action his own not only in the causal sense that it is within his own power and voluntary, but in the more narrowly ethical sense that, among such actions, he has deliberately chosen it. An action, to be ethically well done, must proceed from ethical desire as its volitional *arche.* Ethical desire is choice: "[C]hoice would be deliberate desire of things in our own power" *(kai he prohairesis an eie bouleutike orexis ton eph hemin;* E.N. III.3.1113a10–11; cf. VI.2.1139a22–23).

Cognitive control consists in the action's being understood by the agent in all relevant aspects *(nous, dianoia, logos).* It is needed for the action to be in his own power and voluntary, in contrast to being caused by ignorance *(di' agnoian).* And it is needed for the action to be the object of ethical desire or deliberate choice. For since ethical excellence is normative *(E.N.* VI.10.1143a8–9), ethical desire must involve understanding the right rule according to which actions should be done (ἀναγκαῖον ἐπισκέψασθαι τὰ περὶ τὰς πράξεις πῶς πρακτέον αὐτάς . . . τὸ μὲν οὖν κατὰ τὸν ὀρθὸν λόγον πράττειν κοινὸν καὶ ὑποκείσθω; E.N. II.2.1103b29–32).

The necessary involvement of cognitive control in ethical agent-centering is argued repeatedly and reflected in some of Aristotle's distinctive ethical vocabulary. The understanding needed to place an action in the agent's own power is both factual and inferential. He needs to know the particular circumstances of his action *(he kath hekasta en hois . . . he praxis; E.N.* III.1.1110b33–1a1), such as the person acted on, and the action, and the instrument and the purpose, since otherwise the action is a mistake *(hamartema).* But he also needs to be able to make rational inferences from these facts and project a reasonable expectation, since otherwise (if it is beyond reasonable expectation *[paralogos]*) the action is a misadventure *(atychema; E.N.* V.8.1135b11–17).

The understanding needed to make desire ethical is objective ethical knowledge, truth, epitomized in the practically wise or good man: "and perhaps the good man differs from others most by seeing the truth in each class of things, being as it were the norm and measure of them" *(E.N.* III.4.1113a31–33; cf. X.6.1176b24–26 and a15–19). Unlike lesser mortals, what seems pleasant *(hedea)* to him really is so by nature *(physei)*, he understands what generally conduces to the good life *(poia pros to eu zen holos)* and what is good and bad for man *(ta anthropoi agatha kai kaka; E.N. VI.5.1140a24–b7)*. And he knows what is objectively *(einai* in contrast to *phainesthai)* lovable, good, pleasant, and useful *(phileton, agathon, hedy, chresimon; E.N. VIII.2.1155b18–19)*. In ethical knowledge, too, the object is cognitionally prior to the subject, and truth is correspondence. As Sparshott notes:

> For people serious about life, serious people set the standard. What they think right is really right, what they think good is really good. It is not that their dictum establishes what is really good: rather, they see clearly (because they have taken pains to see) what really is the case, both in the world and inwardly in the humanity that they fully and accurately exemplify.[5]

Aristotle coins a distinctive ethical vocabulary to show that only desire *(orexis)* cognitionally guided by ethical truth can be the *arche* of ethical actions:

> [C]hoice is deliberate desire, therefore both the understanding must be true and the desire right, if the choice is to be good, and the former must declare and the latter pursue the same things *(ἡ δὲ προαίρεσις ὄρεξις βουλευτική, δεῖ διὰ ταῦτα μὲν τόν τε λόγον ἀληθῆ εἶναι καὶ τὴν ὄρεξιν ὀρθήν, εἴπερ ἡ προαίρεσις σπουδαία, καὶ τὰ αὐτὰ τὸν μὲν φάναι τὴν δὲ διώκειν). (E.N. VI.2.1139a23–26)*

Such understanding is practical intellect *(he dianoia kai he aletheia praktike; E.N.* VI.2.1139a26–31), which is neither scientific knowledge nor *techne,* but "a true and reasoned practical habit of mind" *(hexin alethe meta logou praktiken; E.N.* VI.5.1140b1–7).

Cognitive control in ethical agent-centering preserves desire from being subjective and ungrounded. Aristotle has therefore woven it into his very terminology:

> The origin of action is choice—its originating rather than its final cause—and the origin of choice is desire and reason with a view to an end. Hence choice is either desiderative reason or ratiocinative desire, and such an origin of action is a man *(πράξεως μὲν οὖν ἀρχὴ προαίρεσις—ὅθεν ἡ κίνησις ἀλλ' οὐχ οὗ ἕνεκα— προαιρέσεως δὲ ὄρεξις καὶ λόγος ὁ ἕνεκά τινος διὸ ἢ*

ὀρεκτικὸς νοῦς ἡ προαίρεσις ἢ ὄρεξις διανοητική, καὶ ἡ
τοιαύτη ἀρχὴ ἄνθρωπος). (E.N. VI.2.1139a31–35)

Moral control consists in the action's deriving its ethical character
from that of the agent. The necessity of this derivation distinguishes
Aristotelian ethics from Socratic intellectualism. For if an action could be
done ethically well if desire were only cognitively guided, knowledge of
ethical truth would guarantee ethically good action. But Aristotle holds
that ethical excellence *(arete ethous)* and intellectual excellence *(arete
dianoias)* are not the same (E.N. VI.1.1138b35–9a1) and that both are required as sources of ethically good actions *(eupraxia, spoudaiai energeiai;
E.N.* X.6.1176b18–19; VI. 2.1139a34–35).

The agent's own ethical excellence *(arete)* is generically a state of
character *(hexis)* rather than a potentiality *(dynamis)*, from which he is a
good man *(aph hes agathos anthropos ginetai; E.N.* II.5.1106a10–6.1106a24).
His own goodness lies in his state of character, so that: "It makes no
difference whether we consider the state of character or the man characterized by it" *(diapherei d'outhen ten hexin e ton kata ten hexin skopein; E.N.*
IV.3.1123b1–2; cf. IV. 1.1120b7–9).

Ethical goodness lies in *hexis,* from which *(aph hes)* the agent derives
his goodness in an adjectival sense (making him a good man), while the
action derives it in an adverbial sense (making him do it ethically well).
The double occurrence of *aph hes* to mark first adjectival and subsequent
to it, adverbial derivation (E.N. II.6.1106a22–24; V.1.1129a6–9) is echoed
in other locutions. The agent *(ho pratton)* must be in a certain condition
when he acts *(hos echon)*, and his own ethical condition must be firm and
unchangeable *(bebaios kai ametakinetos echon; E.N.* II.4.1105a26–33). It is
causally grounding for his acting ethically well, since he does so because
he is ethically good *(toi ten hexin toioutos einai; E.N.* IV.7.1127b1–3; *kata ten
hexin gar kai toi toiosde einai;* IV.7.1127b15; *to hodi echonta tauta poein;*
V.9.1137a21–26). Moral control in ethical agent-centering turns doing unjust
actions accidentally into acting unjustly: "for to do what is unjust is not
the same as to act unjustly" *(ou gar tauton to t'adika prattein toi adikein;
E.N.* V.9.1136a25–28).

To sum up: the central focus in ethical living is the agent *(ho pratton)*,
from whose own condition *(pos echon,* in which all four dimensions of
control are closely interwoven) the ethical character of his actions is
derived. Ethical agent-centering is complex and well balanced among
causal, volitional, cognitive, and moral aspects. Ethical action is corre-
spondingly derivative in all these aspects. In its functional role and
categorial status, and hence in its descriptive content (both structurally
and qualitatively), it is posterior to the agent, who is the *ousia.*

This is what Aristotle's characterization of life as being structured
around one person *(peri hena)* means in *Poetics* 8. This is the life of which

art is generically an imitation (*mimesis* 2). But in terms of Aristotle's central *aporia*, this is the life that art cannot imitate in its agent-centered structure. For a tragic action is not agent-centered. Conversely, an ethical action is not tragic.

4.1.2 Object-Centering (Tragic Action)

Poetics 8 contrasts this *peri hena* structure of life with the *peri mian praxin* structure of art. The contrast is mutually exclusive. A tragic action is unlike an ethical action in functional role and categorial status and hence also in descriptive content (structurally and qualitatively). None of the four dimensions of control that are involved in ethical agent-centering apply to it. Its tragic qualitative nature *(poion)* is adjectival rather than adverbial *(tragikon* rather than *tragikos).*

A preliminary clarification may be in order. As argued at the end of chapter 2, a tragedy is an *ousia* because it could not be a *pros hen* dependent accidental attribute of either its producer (the playwright) or its recipient (a reader or theatre audience). Tragic action must therefore be carefully distinguished both from the playwright's productive activity of writing the tragedy and from the tragedy's transeunt effect on an audience. It is intrinsic to the tragedy itself as one of its six constitutive parts, its *mythos*. And since a tragedy is an *ousia*, an object, tragic action is object-centered. Its functional role and categorial status and hence its descriptive content are determined by its relationship with the tragedy itself. They are not derivative from any *ousia* (either playwright or audience) extrinsic to the tragedy.

The relationship of the tragic action with the tragedy is indicated in *Poetics* 8 as being the focus around which the tragedy is structured *(peri mian praxin)*. As such, its functional role is to be the tragedy's causally constitutive *arche* (formal-final cause, compositional principle) in the primary category of *ousia*. The action's commensurate descriptive content is structurally a stringent complex unity and qualitatively the pitiful and fearsome, both together making it tragic. As the *peri hena/peri mian praxin* of *Poetics* 8 indicates, the action's functional role and categorial status, as also its descriptive content, are not derivative from an agent intrinsic to the tragedy (a protagonist or protagonists) any more than from any extrinsic *ousia*. Tragic action is not derivative from anything at all but rather constitutively prior to the tragedy, its *arche hoion psyche*.

4.1.3 Comparison of Ethical and Tragic Action

On every point of comparison, ethical and tragic action are not only different but incompatible. Their respective functional roles place them in different categories *(poiein* and *ousia*, respectively), and their consequent descriptive contents can be structurally contrasted in the spatial meta-phors of a finitely circular and a finitely straight line.[6] The former has no parts *(mere)* different from the whole and from each other in form *(eidei)*. It is not temporally successive *(ephexes)*, has no internal links of efficient causality *(dia)*, and is complete at every moment. The latter has parts *(mere)* different from the whole and from each other in form *(eidei)*. It is temporally successive *(ephexes, met' allela)*, has internal links of efficient causality *(di' allela)*, and is complete only at its end *(teleuten)*.

The descriptive contents of ethical and tragic action can be qualita-tively compared only by contrast: an ethical action is adverbially good *(eu)*, a tragic action is adjectivally tragic *(tragikon, eleeinon kai phoberon)*. The ethical quality of the former is derivative from the agent, while the tragic quality of the latter is intrinsic to itself. The former is not tragic, because *to tragikon* is art-specific. The latter could not be ethical, because the norm and measure of ethical excellence, the practically wise man, is not applicable to a tragedy. A tragic action not only is not, but could not be, done as a practically wise man would do it. To sum up: an ethical action is derivative from the agent functionally, categorially, and in de-scriptive content, while a tragic action is not.

Aristotle contrasts art and life in *E.N.* I. 7–10 with specific reference to tragedy and epic. The contrast shows that none of the four dimensions of control in ethical agent-centering apply to a tragic action. Causal con-trol does not apply: ethical action is under the agent's causal control because it is an internal good, a good of the soul rather than an external one. Hence, it is largely (though not entirely) independent of external factors and of what happens or befalls, including radical changes of for-tune. These are marginalized as mere additions to life *(prosdeitai)*, which do not affect the ethical quality of actions nor success in life nor happi-ness. Aristotle distinguishes the happy man *(eudaimon)* from the blessed man *(makarios)*, though commentators differ on this point.[7] Tragic action, by contrast, is not under the agent's (the protagonist or protagonists) causal control, because it is not internal but external, what happens or befalls *(pragmata, pathemata)*, which paradigmatically includes a radical change of fortune *(peripeteia, eutychia, dystychia)*. What is marginal in ethi-cal action is central in tragic action. Causal agent-control is replaced by causal action-control, since the parts of the complex tragic action stand in a relationship of sequential efficient causality *(met' allela* and *di' allela)*, and the agent suffers the results *(pathemata)* of this self-contained action-causality.

Volitional control does not apply: ethical action is under the agent's volitional control, because he desires it for its own sake and with delib-erate choice as a good. Tragic action, by contrast, is not under the agent's volitional control because he does not desire it nor deliberately choose it as a good.

Cognitive control does not apply: ethical action is under the agent's cognitive control because he understands it in all relevant factual and inferential aspects. Tragic action, by contrast, is not under the agent's cognitive control because he does not know relevant factual (e.g., *hamartia* of kin relationships) nor inferential aspects *(para doxan)*.

Moral control does not apply: ethical action is under the agent's moral control because its ethical character is derived from his. Tragic action, by contrast, is not under the agent's moral control because ethical characters *(ethe)* are secondary and not causally effective. The action is not caused, e.g., by bad character *(dia kakian kai mochtherian)* but by ignorance *(di' hamartian, di' agnoian)*.

Aristotle asks whether a tragedy's or epic's focus on the action with its change of fortune is not altogether wrong *(oudamos orthon)*. Wrong for what? Clearly not for a tragedy or epic, which it "besouls." Wrong, then, from the perspective of ethical living. The *Poetics* 8 contrast of *peri hena* and *peri mian praxin* is such that the latter is altogether wrong as a mirror of the former. There is little that art can teach us about life, and so its significance and meaning cannot be didactic.

Can *mimesis* 2 survive this wrongness as a viable generic definition of art? The comparative elucidation of Aristotle's central *aporia* from the texts of *E.N.* and *Poetics* raises serious doubt about his ability to resolve it. Tragic action, re-centered and re-categorized, with a different functional role and descriptive content, bears little similarity to ethical action.

What saves Aristotle's theory of art are the liberties art may not take with its objects of imitation (see Section 3.3.1 above). It may not take into its own representational content objects that have no reality in life at all. A tragedy's objects of imitation *(praxis, ethe, dianoia)* all occur in ethical living and so provide some link of recognizable similarity between art and life. More importantly, art may not contravene all of life's logical and ethical constraints, despite the radical *peri hena/peri mian praxin* restructuring. That restructuring means that the characteristic ethical vocabulary of *E.N.* is absent from the *Poetics*, that the agent *(ho pratton)* is not among the objects of imitation, and that ethical character appears in the plural *(ethe)* rather than in the singular *(ethos)* and disjoined from *dianoia* rather than conjoined with it. But some of the connections between *praxis, ethos, dianoia* survive the restructuring and are preserved—but under a reversed perspective. In ethical living, actions are in character both ethically and noetically from the perspective of the agent as *arche*. In a tragedy, the action must still be in character ethically and noetically *(toi poioi ta poia atta symbainei legein e prattein kata to eikos e to anankaion; Poetics*

9.1451b6–10)—but from the perspective of the action as *arche.* "Being in character" remains under the reversal of perspective.

Is it enough? Aristotle seems inclined to think so. After all, both in life and in art, his philosophy emphasizes the characteristic rather than the idiosyncratic, the paradigmatic rather than the empirical. The coincidence of *toi poioi ta poia* across the generic divide between life and art strikes him as so significant that he declares art to be more serious and more philosophical than history. *Ex Aristotele,* he can resolve his central *aporia,* since what matters to the sturdiness of *mimesis* 2 is not the quantity of similarities but their significance.

Entering polemical engagement at this point, we may ask: is the mirror-of-life didactic exegesis of the *Poetics* vindicated? Yes and no. Yes, because preserving a viable sense of *mimesis* 2 is bound up with the "being in character" that is common to life and art. No, because a tragedy is a new *ousia* in a subject genus of its own, which relates to nature by *mimesis* 1, and whose artistic significance is therefore intrinsic and constitutive rather than didactic. *Mimesis* 1 is prior to and authoritative for *mimesis* 2. The *peri hena/peri mian praxin* restructuring shows how *mimesis* 1 is achieved via *mimesis* 2 in an art-specific manner.

My polemical contribution to the mirror-of-life didactic exegesis is the reminder that Aristotle differs from Plato. A good painting of a bed is not an ontologically third-rate *bed* but an ontologically first-rate *painting.*[8] The fact that it must be recognizably *of* a bed is an element in and serves its being as a painting. Aristotle, unlike Kandinsky, would have said that it cannot be a great painting unless it is significantly *mimetic* (2) of the characteristic features of a bed. Yet what it can teach us about beds is consequent upon and secondary to what it can teach us about art. For an artistic object is not a teaching aid, it has a definitory artistic nature of its own, its own integral being and *ousia*-hood. To understand that, the *Poetics* must be read in the light of the *Metaphysics,* which sets out the constitutive structure of an *ousia* and thereby the meaning of *mimesis* 1. But in order to understand *mimesis* 2, the *Poetics* must also be read both in contrast to and in the light of *E.N.,* in order to comprehend both the depth of the reversal of perspective and the depth of what survives it as significant *mimetic* (2) representational content.

4.2 Patient-Centering and Object-Centering (Rhetorical and Tragic Action)

4.2.1 Patient-Centering (Rhetorical Action)

Rhetorical action is the act of public speaking, *logos* in the verbal sense of *legein* and *eipein,* which consists of speaker and speech and audience (σύγκειται μὲν γὰρ ἐκ τριῶν ὁ λόγος, ἔκ τε τοῦ λέγοντος καὶ περὶ οὗ λέγει καὶ πρὸς ὄν, καὶ τὸ τέλος πρὸς τοῦτόν ἐστιν, λέγω δὲ τὸν ἀκροατήν; *Rhetoric* I.3.1358a37–b2). This triangular analysis of public speaking focuses on the activity of rhetorical speechmaking in its public setting, on *rhetorike techne* in action. The designation of the speaker as *rhetor* or *ho legon* is complementary to that of the audience as *akroates* or *ho akouon*, showing that rhetoric is essentially action, public performance comparable to the professional actor's or the rhapsode's *techne*, to *hypokrisis* or *rhapsodia* (*Rhetoric* III.7.1408a19–25). As is true of the latter two *technai*, *lexis* in the sense of delivery is therefore an essential part of rhetorical techne: "Our next subject will be delivery *(lexis)*. For it is not enough to know what one should say *(ha dei legein)*, it is necessary to know as well how to say it *(hos dei eipein)*" (*Rhetoric* III.1.1403b14–18). Since *hos dei eipein* includes the use of the voice *(en tei phonei, pos autei dei chresthai)*, *lexis* as delivery is part of rhetorical *techne*, which is the craft of public speaking, of an action.

Aristotle strengthens the parallel of the professional actor's or rhapsode's *techne* with that of the *rhetor* by calling public speaking a contest *(agon)* comparable to a public dramatic or rhapsodic contest *(agon)*, in which prizes *(athla)* are won by those who master *lexis*. *Lexis* may in these contexts be more potent than content (*Rhetoric* III.1.1403b22–4a13). So while poetical *techne* concerns the composition of a tragedy or epic and is distinct from the actor's or rhapsode's *techne*, rhetorical *techne* encompasses both the composition and delivery of a speech. Even if a *rhetor* were to employ a speechwriter *(logographos)*, the latter would have to compose the *logos* with a view to the action of public speaking. *Logos* therefore occurs in two senses, as the speech and the speaking. It is the latter, the "rhetorical performance," that is the basic analysandum of Aristotle's *Rhetoric*, and the former is but one part or aspect of it.[9]

The reason for this focus on rhetorical action is that only one of its three constituents *(synkeitai men ek trion)* is its definitory *telos*, and this *telos* is the audience, which is extrinsic to the speech *(kai to telos pros touton estin, lego de ton akroaten)*. The triangular analysis of rhetorical action subordinates speaker and topic to the audience as their definitory *telos*. The very *raison d'être* of rhetoric is the production of persuasion *(pistis)* in the audience, which leads it to make a decision or judgment *(krisis)*. Rhetorical action is patient-centered, because it is defined in terms of its causal effect on the audience, which is its patient in the general categorial sense of being causally affected *(paschein)*. The causality involved is transeunt efficient causality, and the effect produced is a new accidental condition (a *pistis*) in an already existing natural *ousia* (or rather, *ousiai*). Rhetorical speechmaking is analogous to medical treatment and, like the latter, achieves its patient-centered causal effect only as action.[10]

Aristotle stresses the analogy both in the *E.N.* and in the *Rhetoric*: "For a doctor does not deliberate whether he shall heal, nor a *rhetor* whether he shall persuade . . . but assuming the end *(to telos)*, they investigate how and by what means *(pos kai dia tinon)* it will come about" (*E.N.* III.3.1112b12–16; *Rhetoric* I.1.1355b10–13; I.2.1356b30–35). Both patient-centered *technai* reason back from their respective definitory ends through a chain of causally effective means until they reach a first cause *(to proton aition)*, which is last in the order of analysis but first in the order of becoming *(kai to eschaton en tei analysei proton einai en tei genesei; E.N.* III.3.1112b12–24).

Medical *techne* is the most illuminating analogue of rhetorical *techne* because both are patient-centered in the same way. Both have as their definitory *telos* the production of a new accidental condition in an already existing natural *ousia* (or *ousiai*), rather than the production of a new *ousia*. For both, the product is different from and beyond *(heteron kai para)* the activity of producing it, so that they are *technai* rather than *praxeis*. For both, their *techne* in its theoretical aspect comprises general principles, while causal effect is exerted only in actual public speaking or actual medical treatment toward *(pros)* an individual audience or patient (*Rhetoric* I.2.1356b30–35; 1355b10–34). Both are remedial, coming into play only on special negative occasions, when public decisions must be taken without adequate epistemic guidance (*Rhetoric* I.2.1357a1–4) or when someone is ill. Ideally, neither *rhetors* nor doctors would be needed; realistically, both are needed. Even though rhetorical *techne* is carried out in a public setting toward a mass audience and medical *techne* privately toward an individual patient, their common patient-centered definition determines their function, categorial status, and descriptive content (structurally and qualitatively) in an analogous manner.[11]

Each one's functional role is determined by its patient-centered *telos*, its *hou heneka* or good. Any aspect of a *rhetor's* or a doctor's action is rhetorical or medical only in as far as it is directed toward this *telos*. And it is evaluated as rhetorically or medically good in terms of its causal efficacy with regard to this *telos*. Rhetorical and medical *techne* have their own standards of rightness. But these are patient-centered, unlike the agent-centered standards of ethical rightness or the object-centered standards of artistic rightness (cf. *E.N.* V.9.1137a21–26).

Since rhetorical and medical action are remedial, patient-centering gears them to the particular dysfunctions of their respective patients. A *rhetor* will not persuade an audience, whose lack of adequate epistemic guidance is due to an inability to follow a lengthy train of reasoning, by setting out a string of *enthymemes* and eschewing the techniques of *ethos*, *pathos*, and *lexis* (*Rhetoric* III.8.1419a17–19; II.1.1377b22–31; III.1.1403b22–4a8; III.14.1415a38–b6). The medical analogy is obvious. *Rhetors* and doctors engage in the activities of their respective crafts toward patients as they find them: "It is clear that such introductions are not addressed to ideal hearers, but to hearers as we find them" (*hoti de pros ton akroaten ouch heiper [ho] akroates, delon; Rhetoric* III.14.1415b17–18).

Patient-centering places rhetorical action into the secondary (actually, tertiary) category of the relative (*pros ti*), as it does its medical analogue. It has the categorial status of a means to an end extrinsic to itself: "Things are relative (*pros ti*) . . . as that which can heat to that which can be heated . . . and in general the active to the passive" (*Met.* V. 1020b26–32). Its good (*t'agathon*) and standard of rightness (*to eu*) derive to it from its end in a highly prescriptive manner. Just as it cannot be defined apart from its end, so it cannot be good or be done well apart from its end. The language of the *Rhetoric* is as prescriptive as that of *E.N.* and *Poetics,* for centering their respective actions on an *ousia* provides each with its distinctive focus of prescriptivity. There is a good textual basis for comparing rhetorical with ethical and tragic action, because the prescriptive language marks the *Rhetoric* as genuine Aristotelian doctrine, not as an empirical compilation of current rhetorical practices. The text frequently uses terms such as "ought" (*dei*) or "must" (*chre*) or "necessity" (*ananke*), superlatives or comparatives, the future indicative, *telos* or *ergon,* the normative genitive (e.g., it behoves the *rhetor [tes rhetorikes estin]*), and imperatives.

The categorial status of rhetorical action as *pros ti* is analogous to that of medical action, since both are relative to their respective patients. Rhetorical action is *pros pistin* (or *krisin*) of an audience, medical action *pros hygieian* of an individual patient (e.g., *Rhetoric* I.1.1355b10–13; I.8.1365b21–24). The causal language of datives, of *dia, poiein, ek, dynamis* (in the sense of power to affect), *kataskeuazein,* and *agein* marks them as transeuntly efficient causal means to an end extrinsic to themselves, and such means fall into the category of *pros ti.* This determines their good (*t'agathon*) to be the useful (*to chresimon*) and their standard of rightness (*to eu*) to be causal effectiveness (e.g., *Rhetoric* I.2.1356b18–20; I.1.1355a21–b11; II.18.1391b7; III.16.1416b34–7a3). As *E.N.* makes clear, the good is spoken in all categories, and in that of *pros ti* it is the useful, because ends are good in themselves but means only on account of and for the sake of their ends (*E.N.* I. 6,7). And always the final cause is predominant over the transeuntly efficient (*Physics* II.3).

In its theoretical aspect, rhetoric is a *methodos,* a set of techniques. These are the *pisteis* or *pithana* in the sense of, and usually translated as, means or modes of persuasion:

> Let us now try to give an account of this technique, how and by what means we shall be able to succeed in our objectives . . . and let us define what it is. . . . Let rhetoric be defined as the faculty of observing in any given case

the available means of persuasion. For this is the work of no other craft *(περὶ δὲ αὐτῆς ἤδη τῆς μεθόδου πειρώμεθα λέγειν, πῶς τε καὶ ἐκ τίνων δυνησόμεθα τυγχάνειν τῶν προκειμένων . . . ὁρισάμενοι αὐτὴν τίς ἐστι. . . . Ἔστω δὴ ἡ ῥητορικὴ δύναμις περὶ ἕκαστον τοῦ θεωρῆσαι τὸ ἐνδεχόμενον πιθανόν. τοῦτο γὰρ οὐδεμιᾶς ἑτέρας ἐστὶ τέχνης ἔργον).* (*Rhetoric* I.1.1355b22–27)

Patient-centering determines these techniques not only in their functional role and categorial status but also in their descriptive content. It does so by tailoring them to particular audiences with their particular tasks and dysfunctions. Rhetoric is divided into three types, as determined by three types of audiences: "The hearer *(akroaten)* must be either an observer or a judge about things past or future . . . therefore there must be three types *(gene)* of rhetorical speeches, political, forensic, epideictic" (*Rhetoric* I.3.1358b2–8; cf. a36–37). Each type of audience has the task of making a decision in its own sphere of responsibility; a political one must decide on a collective course of future action, a forensic one on the justice of someone's past action, an epideictic one on the honor due to someone. These tasks determine the respective *tele* of the three types of rhetoric: "The *telos* of each of these is different, and since there are three types of rhetoric, there are three *tele*. For the political *rhetor* it is the advantageous and harmful . . . for forensic ones it is the just or unjust . . . for the epideictic ones who praise and attack a man it is the noble and the shameful" (*Rhetoric* I.3.1358b20–29).

The respective tasks of the three types of audiences enter thematically into the subject matter *(peri hou)* of the three types of rhetoric, since the definitory *telos* of each of the latter is to affect its audience's decision by persuasion: "Since the use of persuasive speech is to lead to decision" (*Epei de he ton pithanon logon chresis pros krisin esti; Rhetoric* II.18.1391b7). The subordination of speaker and speech to the hearer in Aristotle's triangular analysis of rhetorical action is not merely the general *telic* structure of rhetoric, it means that a given type of rhetorical speech is thematically bound to a given type of audience. Thematic dependence or derivation not only imports a definite subject domain but the rhetorical stance of advocacy. For each type of audience aims at a good in the decision it must make, a political audience at the advantageous, a forensic one at the just, an epideictic one at the noble. Hence, the pregiven *(prokeimenon) telos* of each type of rhetoric is to persuade its audience that what the *rhetor* advocates is advantageous, just, or noble: "Since therefore in each type of rhetoric the pregiven *telos* is different" (*Rhetoric* II.18.1391b22–23).

Patient-centering determines the descriptive content of each type of rhetorical action not only thematically and as advocacy, but also to some extent influences how this advocacy is to be carried out. To give but a few examples from political speechmaking: since a political audience aims at the advantageous, political rhetoric must persuade it that the decision advocated by the *rhetor* is in its own interest. This is "most important and effective *(megiston de kai kyriotaton hapanton)* towards being able to persuade ... for all are persuaded by the advantageous" *(Rhetoric* I.8. 1365b21–24). Appeals to the just or the noble are less effective. And lest the audience suspect the *rhetor's* self-interest in the guise of the public good, it is most important *(malista men en tais symboulais ... chresimoteron eis tas symboulas)* for him to use *ethos* as a means of persuasion so as to make himself appear as a man of a certain character *(poion tina phainesthai ton legonta)*, who is well disposed toward his hearers. It is also important to use *pathos* in order to put his hearers in a certain frame of mind *(diakeisthai pos; Rhetoric* II.1.1377b24–30). This strategy, by contrast, would almost certainly backfire in forensic and epideictic rhetoric, which must at least pay lip service to the predominance of the just and the noble.

The deployment of arguments *(enthymemes)*, character *(ethos)*, emotion *(pathos)*, and delivery *(lexis)* as means of persuasion *(Rhetoric* I.2.1356a1–4; III.1) is thus partly determined by the type of audience, but partly also by the particular dysfunctions of a given audience. These may be both intellectual and moral, and Aristotle throughout the text uses fairly strong language in describing them: intellectually, audiences may be incapable of taking a complicated argument in at a glance or of following a long chain of reasoning (I.2.1357a1–4), they may have a weakminded tendency to listen to what is beside the point (III.14.1415a38–b6), they may not be able to follow a series of questions (III.18.1419a17–19), they may fallaciously take the truth of what they know as evidence for the truth of what they do not know (III.16.1417b2–3), mistake apparent proof for proof (I.2.1356a2–4), or draw a false inference about the truth of what a speaker says because they feel the same way about the matter as he (III.7.1408a19–25), they may enjoy having their own notions expressed as if they were universal truths (II.21.1395b1–12). Morally, audiences may, because of bad political institutions, be swayed more by a *rhetor's* enacted delivery than by his arguments (III.1), and they may enjoy having their preconceived values confirmed (II.1.1377b17–20; I.9.1367b7–12). These dysfunctions may make them gullible so as to be persuaded by what seems rather than by what is, and even by what is false (II.5.1383a8–9; II.21.1395a8–9), as long as the speaker hides what he is doing *(lanthanon de poiei;* III.16.1417b8).

Aristotle presents this list of dysfunctions as partly causally determinative of the descriptive content of rhetoric (*dia* in the sense of final causality). Persuasion has to be produced in audiences that are always bad in some way (*pros phaulon gar akroaten; Rhetoric* III.14.1415b5–6; *dia ten tou akroatou mochterian; Rhetoric* III.1.1404a7–8). That, in fact, is its *ergon* (*Rhetoric* I.2.1357a1–4). Hence, the parts (*mere*) and the order (*taxis*) of rhetorical speeches must be adapted to each audience (*Rhetoric* III.16–19). Means to an end have no intrinsic independent principle that would determine their descriptive content structurally (*mere* and *taxis*), i.e., they have no intrinsic formal cause. Patient-centering determines rhetorical means in remarkable detail in thematic and structural dependence. For in any means-end relation, the end as final cause determines the means as efficient cause, and the analogy of rhetorical and medical action holds.

Patient-centering also determines the descriptive content of rhetorical action qualitatively, as persuasive (*pithanon*), since the definitory *telos* of producing persuasion in an audience makes what is subjectively believable prior to what is objectively worthy of belief. In rhetoric, what is *pithanon* is *pithanon* to somebody, on pain of being rhetorically inoperative: "since what is persuasive is persuasive to somebody" (*epei gar to pithanon tini pithanon esti; Rhetoric* I.2.1356b28). The rhetorical order of priority between *pithanon* and *tini pithanon* stands in sharp contrast to Aristotle's normal *epistemic* order of priority, it is in fact the reversal of the latter. Rhetoric reverses Aristotle's cognitional priority of the object by making the subject (the audience) prior to the object (the objective truth). Commentators who try to soften the harshness of this reversal echo Aristotle's own uneasiness. But the location of the definitory *telos*, the production of persuasion, in the audience leaves little scope for softening.[12]

That is all the more so because the remedial character of rhetorical action accepts the dysfunctions of a given audience as determinative, in fact panders to them and so confirms and strengthens them. All versions of "praising the Athenians to the Athenians" cannot but make the Athenians more Athenian. Rhetoric aims at producing persuasion in audiences as it finds them rather than at reforming audiences. The *rhetor qua rhetor* is neither an educator nor a statesman. His *techne* is distinct and cannot approximate too far to any other *techne* or *episteme* without destroying its own nature (*lesetai ten physin auton; Rhetoric* I.4.1359b12–16). Rhetoric may therefore have not only questionable means but a questionable definitory end as well. The objective goodness of a successfully produced persuasion in an audience is beyond the purview of rhetoric *qua* rhetoric. The rhetorical reversal of Aristotle's normal *epistemic* stance is also a reversal of his normal ethical stance, in which what is good is normative for what seems so.[13]

At this point the analogy between rhetorical and medical action, which has held so far, breaks down. For while the remedial character of medical action also accepts patients as it finds them and adapts its means to their dysfunctions, it does not pander to them nor accept them as final. It aims at freeing patients from them, and therefore health is not a questionable definitory end. Achieved health is good, while achieved rhetorical persuasion may only seem so. The *Rhetoric* is filled with directives to the *rhetor* to produce *(poiein) pros doxan*, the persuasive and the seemingly persuasive *(to pithanon kai to phainomenon pithanon)*, to prove or seem to prove *(dia tou deiknynai e phainesthai deiknynai)*, to make himself and his speech seem to be of a certain character *(toioutoi phanountai kai autoi kai hoi logoi) (Rhetoric* III.1.1404a1–3; I.1.1355b15–17; I.2.1356a2–4; II.13.1390a26–27). The distance between *einai* and *phainesthai* marks the disanalogy between the definitory *tele* of medicine and rhetoric. For to produce seeming rather than real health would be medical malpractice, while to produce a persuasion of seeming goodness or validity is successful rhetorical practice.

To sum up: the definitory focus of rhetorical action is on the patient *(ho akroates, ho akouon),* to whom Aristotle's triangular analysis subordinates speaker *(ho legon)* and speech *(peri hou).* Patient-centering determines rhetorical action in its functional role, its categorial status, and its descriptive content, making it derivative from the patient in all these respects. The patient is prior as the *ousia* to whom rhetorical action is posterior. The standard of excellence of rhetorical *techne* is therefore also derivative and posterior, consisting in the useful *(to chresimon)* in the sense of transeunt efficient causality. Therefore, rhetoric is generically defined as a *dynamis,* a causally effective power. It is *techne* in the sense of technique.

Rhetorical action as structured around the patient (one might say: *peri akroaten)* is not mentioned in *Poetics* 8, which contrasts only the *peri hena* structuring around one agent of ethical living with the *peri mian praxin* structuring around one action of art. It is not mentioned because it is not relevant. Art is neither patient-centered nor an imitation *(mimesis* 2) of rhetoric. Its definitory similarity and differentiation is with, and from, agent-centering.

4.2.2 Comparison of Rhetorical and Tragic Action

The contrast between the patient-centered structure of rhetoric and the object-centered structure of art is mutually exclusive. For the distance between rhetorical action in the tertiary category of *pros ti* and tragic action in the primary category of *ousia* is the greatest categorial distance in Aristotle's thought-world. The integrity of his thought-world depends on their mutual exclusiveness. Relegating *pros ti* to tertiary status is his first line of defense against the still looming threat of the Parmenidean oneness of being and against the outmoded Platonic attempt in the *Sophist* to deal with it by giving *kath hauto* and *pros ti* equal meta-ontological status. Aristotle safeguards the integrity of substantial being by not allowing *pros ti* to enter constitutively into the being of any entitative *ousia* and so to be prior to it. For *pros ti* is *hetero-telic* while *ousia* is *auto-telic*.

Rhetorical patient-centering is therefore not only incompatible with the object-centering of art but is a threat to its *auto-telic* integrity. A work of art has an intrinsic definitory *telos*, an intrinsic standard of excellence, and it is a self-referential, self-significant, and self-worthy analogue of a living animal. Nowhere does Aristotle apply the triangular analysis of rhetorical speechmaking to art. Nor does he ever definitorily subordinate a tragedy to an audience. For if he did, actual rather than appropriate audience response would be normative. As medical treatment is definitorily directed to the health *(pros hygieian)* of a patient as the doctor finds him, and rhetorical speechmaking is definitorily directed to the persuasion *(pros pistin)* of a patient as the *rhetor* finds it, so a tragedy would be definitorily directed to the katharsis or pleasure or emotion *(pros katharsin or pros hedonen or pros pathos)* of a patient as the playwright finds it, with all that that would entail.

The threat to art posed by assimilating it to rhetorical patient-centering is clear. It would render works of art definitorily *hetero-telic* and hence reduce them to the status of means to the end of producing new accidental conditions in recipients, be these ends didactic, hedonistic, moralistic, therapeutic, or a mixture of any of these. The issue between art and rhetoric is not whether works of art can causally affect a recipient, it is only whether that effect is its definitory *telos*. Aristotle's categories allow him to give full scope to its accidental transeunt causal effects while safeguarding the essential *auto-telic* integrity of a work of art.

The distance between object- and patient-centering becomes clear when one considers the role of the audience in art and in rhetoric. Aristotle entertains no higher opinion of a tragic than of a rhetorical audience but refers to both in largely pejorative terms. This gives one a fair basis of comparison. In art, the audience is optional rather than necessary, since a tragedy is not composed with a view to performance *(pros ta theatra)* but according to the standard of the finest tragedy *(he kata ten technen kalliste tragodia)*. Therefore the actor's *techne (hypokrisis)* is distinct from the playwright's *(poietike)*. Nor is a tragedy remedial. Reference to the audience is almost always introduced by expressions such as "in addition to" *(pros toutois)*, "next" *(eita)*, and "sign" *(semeion)*, which indicates that it is additional to, or an empirical confirmation of, an already completed argument. Audience reaction is posterior to the tragedy *(apo tes tragodias)* and measured by the tragedy itself as the norm of its appropriateness. A playwright who gears his *techne* to the preferences or weaknesses of an audience will produce a bad tragedy. The audience does not enter constitutively into the functional role, categorial status, or descriptive content of tragic action.

By contrast, in rhetoric the audience is necessary, since in Aristotle's triangular analysis speaker and speech are subordinated to it as definitory *telos.* Rhetorical *techne* therefore includes performance, and hence speeches are composed with a view to public enactment, which is akin to *hypokrisis* and *rhapsodia.* And rhetoric is remedial, like medicine. References to the audience are not (I believe never) introduced by expressions such as *pros toutois, eita, semeion.* They are part of the argument itself. Audience reaction is prior to rhetorical speechmaking and is the measure of its success. A *rhetor* who gears his *techne* to the preferences and weaknesses of an audience will produce good, i.e., effective, rhetoric. The audience enters constitutively into the functional role, categorial status, and descriptive content of rhetorical action, analogously to the way in which the patient enters into medical action.

The reason for this divergent role of the audience in art and in rhetoric is that the product of art is a tragedy, while that of rhetoric is persuasion in a given audience. For both are, as *technai,* determined by, and understood in terms of, their respective products.

I have included the comparison of tragic and rhetorical action in this study purely for polemical reasons. My approach *ex Aristotele* gives no textual warrant for understanding a tragedy as definitorily patient-centered. Aristotle in *Poetics* 25 explicitly differentiates poetical *techne* from rhetorical and ascribes to it an intrinsic standard of rightness *(orthotes)* generically grounded in imitation *(mimetos)* and pertaining to the tragedy itself. The above clarification of the relationship of the two texts prepares the ground for polemical engagement.

Having reached this point, I must confess to some unease. For my polemical contribution is blunt. It consists in suggesting that the *Poetics* should not be read in the light of the *Rhetoric* at all, certainly not definitorily, but not even in the sense that the causal effect of a tragedy on a recipient might be understood in terms of the *Rhetoric.* For the latter calculates the effects of its means of persuasion piecemeal, while the former's effect is appropriate *(oikeion)* only if the tragedy is received as an integral whole *(Poetics* 23.1459a17–21). A *rhetor* who adapts his means of persuasion to the audience is a good *rhetor.* A playwright who adapts the six constitutive parts of a tragedy to anything but the tragedy as a unified whole is a bad playwright. Criticism in the sense of the analytical dismemberment of a work of art in terms of audience reaction would be unacceptable to Aristotle.

This unqualified rejection of the *Rhetoric* as relevant to understanding the *Poetics* faces some textual and some historical opposition. Textually, there are parallels, particularly in Aristotle's discussion of the emotions *(pathe)*. These clearly are relevant. For human emotions are the same in art and in rhetoric. My rejection rather pertains to assimilating the role of emotive factors in a tragedy to their role in rhetorical speechmaking. For in object-centering they are objective as qualitative aspects of the descriptive content of tragic action. The object, the tragedy itself, is emotively prior to the audience's subjectively felt emotion. But in patient-centering *pathos* is one of the means of persuasion, which makes the audience's subjectively felt emotion prior. Object- and patient-centering do not change the content of emotion, but they do change its role and the focus of its priority.

Historically, my blunt rejection faces a long-established exegetical tradition to the contrary. This has focused on categorizing *katharsis* in the formal definition of tragedy as *pros ti* to the audience. While it still persists, some commentators are taking *katharsis* to have an intrinsic rather than extrinsic reference. Scholars such as Halliwell and McKeon have admirably elucidated and criticized the *rhetorizising* exegetical tradition.[14] I should therefore like to offer a different kind of polemical contribution.

The *rhetorizising* categorization of *katharsis* in *Poetics* 6 as *pros ti* to the audience may seem *prima facie* reasonable, and the text is too condensed and syntactically unperspicacious at this point to decide the issue authoritatively. What I hope can decide it is working out the implications of patient-centering, such as this study has attempted. For if one understands *katharsis* as patient-centered, one must accept all the implications of this centering. Since an Aristotelian formal definition cannot be in more than one category, least of all both in those of *ousia* and *pros ti*, a tragedy as a whole would thereby be definitorily categorized as *pros ti*. This would transfer to it all that pertains to rhetorical speechmaking, which need not be repeated here.

Not only would this contradict the generic definition of art as imitation *(mimesis* 2) (see Section 3.1.3 above), it would be incompatible with the overwhelming evidence of the text and dismaying to all lovers of art who are concerned to safeguard its *auto-telic* dignity. My polemical contribution to the *Poetics-Rhetoric* debate is, in short, that object- and patient-centering are strongly mutually exclusive, so that a tragedy as a whole must be definitorily one or the other, but not both. And it is the former definitorily, the latter only accidentally.

CONCLUSION

The approach of this study has been an attempt to understand the *Poetics* *ex Aristotele* by gradual adumbration from ever narrowing parameters of Aristotelian philosophy. As noted, such an adumbration requires choices and hence is debatable at every level. *Ex Aristotele*, the study's heuristic principle, is never accessible uncontroversially. But neither is it ever dispensable lest the designation "Aristotelian" be used lightly. The focus on questions of approach has been deliberate and sustained, precisely because it is debatable at every level. This study is meant to be a contribution to and stimulus for explicit, sustained metalevel reflection and debate. Our paradoxical situation is that metalevel decisions concerning the relevant parameters of the reception of ancient texts are prior to text establishment, translation, and exegesis. Yet they must gradually grow out of a scholar's object-level engagement with the text and so be posterior, on pain of imposing an alien framework on it. What is prior by nature is posterior in relation to us.

How then does the *Poetics* appear from this attempt at an *ex Aristotele* approach? The three modes of centering (agent, patient, object) are ways in which Aristotle's world is ordered. Both constitutive principles *(archai)* and accidents *(symbebekota)* must be centered on *synola*, individual entitative *ousiai*, since neither can be separately and independently. His recognition of three different modes of *ousia*-centering gives his world-order a richly differentiated texture and integrates human agency into it.

For while there are no human actions apart from human agents, not all actions are agent-centered.

This means that human agents are not the focus of prescriptivity for all their actions. They clearly are so for their ethical actions, which are derivative from themselves and can be spatially represented as finite circular lines whose origin *(hopothen)* and end *(telos)* coincide in the agent. They are not so for rhetorical actions, which are derivative from their patients and can be spatially represented as finite straight lines whose origin and *telos* diverge, the origin being the agent and the *telos* being the patient. Human agency is definitorily subordinated to the patient-centered focus of prescriptivity. Human agents are not the focus of prescriptivity for tragic actions, which are not derivative from anything but rather constitutively prior to the tragedies on which they are centered. They can be spatially represented as finite straight lines whose beginning *(arche)* and end *(teleute)* diverge, but their beginning is not an agent and their end not a patient. Instead, their beginning and end are themselves actions, parts of the complex tragic action, which thus lies self-contained within its own boundaries, and so is complete and whole. Human agency and human patiency are both subordinated to the object-centered focus of prescriptivity.

The *Poetics* emerges as a text that understands art as object-centered, as definitorily centered on the work of art itself. Its subordination of both human agency and patiency to the tragedy itself as the focus of prescriptivity allows works of art to take their place as genuine substantial beings, *ousiai,* alongside those that nature produces. But while nature produces its *ousiai* without regard to either human agency or patiency, the playwright must produce a tragedy by taking account of them and making them posterior. In life, human *poiein* and *paschein,* doing and being affected, stand in a natural cosmic context, which has its own independent centers of prescriptivity in natural *ousiai.* Man as agent and as patient must live with a natural world that is not ordered according to his subjective wishes and needs, but has its own objective immanent *archai.* The *Poetics* tells us that we must live like this even with things we make ourselves. Our reward is that if we do, these things can be excellent. And perhaps our consolation is that they and their natural analogues are cosmic in their own right.

The playwright's taking account of and subordinating human agency and patiency to the tragedy itself means that there are some constants that hold steady throughout the three modes of centering, when they involve humans. These are the characteristic (rather than idiosyncratic) links between *praxis, ethos,* and *dianoia.* For human action, whether tragic, rhetorical, or ethical, is connected with *ethos* and *dianoia,* so that it is always ethically and noetically in character. The "to a man of such a character such actions" *(toi poioi ta poia)* of art *(Poetics* 9,1451b8), the "what pertains to a man or men of such a character" *(ti toi toioide e tois toioisde)* of rhetoric *(Rhetoric* I.2.1356b30–35), the "actions such as the just or wise man would do" *(toiauta hoia an ho dikaios e ho sophron praxeien)* of ethics *(E.N.* II.4.1105b5–9) preserve these characteristic links even under the radical reversals of perspective of their different modes of centering. Insofar as Aristotle has a concept of a "human world," these constants give it content.

This raises the question whether Aristotle's theory of art could encompass nonrepresentational works, which cannot be generically defined as *mimetic* of human life *(mimesis* 2). Though he had no concept of nonrepresentational art and so could not have formulated this question himself, it seems like a fair final test of the sturdiness of his theory. For if it is bound to a *mimetic* (2) generic definition and so to representational content, it may in an important sense be dated.

Aristotle's generic definition of art as *mimesis* 2 serves three functions. It serves to differentiate artistic from useful *technai,* it serves to locate all works of art in a distinctive subject genus, and it preserves the link of art with human life. Two questions should be asked in order to arrive at a final evaluation of his theory of art. The first is whether something other than a work of art's representational content could serve all three functions within his own philosophy. This is a historical question. The second is whether the three functions are important in any theory of art, and whether they can be preserved at a general level that encompasses both representational and nonrepresentational works. This is a systematic question, which attempts to establish a ground for comparison and evaluation between Aristotle's and any other theory of art.

First the historical question. In Aristotle's thought-world, I believe, nothing else could have served all three functions. For since all *technai* relate to nature by structural or constitutive imitation, *mimesis* 1 could not serve to differentiate artistic from useful *technai.* Since the products of all *technai* in the category of *ousia* are analogues of natural *ousiai,* the analogy (A:B = C:D) could not serve to differentiate one kind of manmade *ousia* from another. In order to effect the differentiation, Aristotle had to have recourse to a different factor. The question then is whether that factor had to be part of the representational content *(mimesis* 2).

I believe that it had to be. For it had to be something shared by all products of artistic *techne* and by no products of useful *techne,* it had to effect a mutually exclusive differentiation. Moreover, that differentiation had to be essential rather than merely accidental, since otherwise the products of artistic and of useful *technai* would be essentially the same. But a mutually exclusive essential differentiation wide enough to encompass a number of specific natures (e.g., painting, sculpture, music, dance, poetry) is generic for Aristotle. The differentiating factor had to be a genus, a qualitative generic nature, which then also served to place all works of art into a distinctive subject genus and so make them definable. The same factor had to serve both the function of differentiating artistic from useful *techne* and of placing all works of art into a distinctive subject genus. Only *mimesis* 2 could do this for him.

The reason lies within the framework of Aristotelian philosophy. What two domains of *ousiai* have in common cannot differentiate them. The substantial products of artistic and of useful *technai* are both man-made, so being man-made cannot differentiate them. Both are analogues of natural *ousiai*, so immanent constitutive lawfulness cannot differentiate them. And neither being man-made nor being *ousiai* can serve as their generic definition, since neither is a subject genus. Aristotle's careful distinction between functional and definitory metaphysical *logoi* means that essential definition cannot be based on reference to constitutive lawfulness as such, but requires reference to qualitative descriptive content (see Section 2.3 above). Generic descriptive content is shared by all the specific natures within a subject genus. In the case of art, it is the descriptive content of the adjective "artistic" in "artistic *techne*." *Techne* is what artistic and useful *ousiai* have in common, artistic is what differentiates the former from the latter. The immanent constitutive lawfulness of works of art must be artistic lawfulness, and it is *mimesis* 2 which gives the adjective "artistic" conceptual content.

That conceptual content lies in the objects of imitation (*mimesis* 2): *praxis, ethe, dianoia*. They provide the generic descriptive qualitative content of works of art, analogously to animal *(zoon)* for human beings. And like *zoon*, they are specifically different in different specific natures (*Met.* X.8). Nothing else than *mimesis* 2 could have done this for Aristotle, precisely because *mimesis* 1 does not itself have qualitative descriptive content and so could not by itself be artistic. Nor could any other factor within a work of art be so. For it would have to be a factor shared by all works of art, yet distinct from *mimesis* 1. It would, if *per impossibile* Aristotle had had a concept of nonrepresentational art, have to be a qualitative factor shared by both representational and nonrepresentational art, and yet distinct from *mimesis* 1. His philosophy did not provide for that possibility.

Mimesis 2, in addition to serving the functions of differentiating artistic from useful *technai* and of placing all works of art within a distinctive subject genus, also preserves the link between art and human life. For note that *mimesis* 1 does not do so. It relates *techne* to *physis* generally, not specifically to human life. The structural or constitutive analogy based on *mimesis* 1 holds between any substantial artifact and any natural *ousia*. Being a product of *techne*, i.e., being man-made, only establishes a link of efficient causality between artifacts and human life, since the *technites* is the maker of the artifact. But in Aristotle's account of *techne,* a substantial product of human making is separate from and beyond the maker *(heteron kai para)* and is to be defined independently of him in terms of its own immanent constitutive formal-final cause. A distinctively artistic link between art and human life therefore has to lie in a work of art's own immanent constitutive formal-final cause, its *arche hoion psyche* and *telos.* That is once more the descriptive content of *mimesis* 2. It makes the link with human life generic and hence essential and definitory. Only representational content could do so.

To answer the historical question: in Aristotle's philosophy with its careful distinction of levels and order of priority, as set out in the schema in Section 2.4 above, qualitative descriptive content is generic and specific *(genos* and *eidos).* Above the highest genera, there is only analogy. What connects *techne* and *physis* generally is only *mimesis* 1, the basis of the analogy between them. *Techne* is therefore not a generic nature and hence not a subject genus. If Aristotle had only *mimesis* 1 and not also *mimesis* 2, he could not have differentiated artistic from useful *technai,* he could not have placed all works of art into a distinctive subject genus and so made them *auto-telically* definable, and he could not have preserved the link of art with human life. He could not have given the adjective "artistic" distinctive conceptual content. The price he has to pay is the inability of his theory of art to encompass nonrepresentational works, a price of which he was not aware. In the sense that we today rightly consider it a desideratum for a theory of art to encompass both representational and nonrepresentational works, Aristotle's theory is dated. *Mimesis* 2 ties art thematically to human life, which we would find intolerably restrictive.

What did he purchase at this price? He gained the systematic embeddedness of his theory of art in his general philosophy, which meant that it was not *ad hoc* but used the same conceptual substantive-methodological constants. That made it not only Aristotelian but intelligible, for *ad hoc* conceptualizations lack intelligibility in terms of continuity with a wider conceptual framework. They are therefore always a philosophical problem. This is one problem he was able to avoid. He also gained an impressive economy by letting one and the same factor *(mimesis* 2) serve all three of the above functions. He was able to differentiate artistic from useful *technai* by giving the adjective "artistic" conceptual content, and this must surely stand as a significant achievement. Making works of art definable saved the domain of art from obscurantism.[1] Preserving the link with human life by incorporating the characteristic human constants *(praxis, ethe, dianoia)* into the generic nature of art and yet restructuring them in an art-specific manner *(peri mian praxin),* is as subtle and profound as anything in the *corpus*. It enabled him to preserve the *auto-telic* independence of the works and yet account for the fact that our engagement with art is different from our engagement with nature as also from our relationship with useful artifacts. What he gained would have seemed to him well worth the price.

Turning now to the systematic question whether the three functions are important in any theory of art, and whether they can be preserved at a general level that encompasses both representational and nonrepresentational works, the answer is less clear-cut. It is *prima facie* likely that they are important. For the adjective "artistic" is vacuous, if the products of artistic *techne* cannot be differentiated from those of useful *techne*. And one does not have a *theory* of art that meets normal philosophical standards of theory-construction, if "artistic" cannot be given conceptual content. Being man-made and being intrinsically lawful are not as such art-specific, since they are true of useful artifacts as well. Placing all works of art into a distinctive subject-genus is Aristotle's way of making them definable, since definition is by genus and differentia for him. That may not be important for all theories of art, since definition may be understood differently. But making works of art definable, in the sense of distinguishing what can be said about them essentially and art-specifically, is still important. For the alternatives are obscurantism or reductionism of various sorts. Preserving the link of art with human life seems to be a perennial concern of theory of art, and the mere fact that a human being is the maker seems inadequate, because it does not account for the fact that our engagement with art differs from our engagement with nature as well as from our relationship with useful artifacts.

If all three functions are important, can they be preserved at a general level, which encompasses both representational and nonrepresentational works? Dealing with this question with reference to a variety of theories of art would go far beyond the bounds of this study. I shall therefore restrict myself to an answer in terms of Kandinsky's theory,[2] because he as a pioneer of nonrepresentational art confronted the problem of giving the adjective "artistic" conceptual content at a comprehensive level. I believe that his theory of art is able to preserve all three functions at that level.

Though he does not explicitly deal with the products of useful *techne*, but rather relates works of art to natural beings, much like Aristotle's *mimesis* 1, he is able to give works of art a distinctive art-specific qualitative content, in terms of which they can be differentiated from useful artifacts. He does so by letting the definitory intrinsic compositional lawfulness of works of art grow out of, and be responsive to, their distinctive materials or means. Since the latter are art-specific, so is the former. Kandinsky solves the most difficult theoretical problem posed by the advent of nonrepresentational painting by giving the painterly means or materials definitory significance, so that the content of art is art for representational and nonrepresentational works alike. For representational content is but one of the painterly means or materials, which a painting may or may not have. But all paintings have point, line, plane, and color and are compositions of these painterly materials. A work of art is therefore a distinctively artistic *auto-telic* microcosm, a new world in its own right, which is not about, and hence not definable in terms of, anything extrinsic. So the adjective "artistic" is given conceptual content.[3]

The first function can be preserved at this general comprehensive level. The same factor that differentiates the products of artistic *techne* from those of useful *techne* also serves the second function of making works of art definable. For the inner responsiveness of compositional lawfulness to the distinctive artistic materials is definitory for the different species of art. This alone is essential, while all else is extrinsic and accidental. Kandinsky bundles all *Hilfswissenschaften* into the domain of the extrinsic and accidental, since none of them is art-specific in its own right. He calls them positive sciences, which deal with the subjective side of art, its "relatively opaque outer skin."[4]

What about the link of art with human life? Kandinsky cannot at this general level preserve it thematically by anything resembling Aristotle's *mimesis* 2, he cannot incorporate any human constants into the definitory nature of a work of art. For neither the painterly materials nor their painterly composition can generally contain anything *mimetic* (2) of human life (though a painting's representational content may do so). The only links Kandinsky can preserve with human life are therefore in terms of what Aristotle would call efficient causality (the fact that a work of art is made by a human being), and in terms of the "relatively opaque outer skin" of works covered by the various *Hilfswissenschaften*. Is it enough to account for the fact that we relate differently to art than to nature and to useful artifacts?

I believe that it is. Kandinsky vacillates about the importance of the extrinsic and accidental "relatively opaque outer skin" of works of art, especially man's spiritual nature.[5] Yet on balance he seems to preserve the *auto-telic* definitory nature of art. But he endows man's efficient causality (man as the maker of the works) with a great deal of content, so that it becomes a distinctive link of art with life. For art, having art-specific materials and hence art-specific qualitative content, actualizes its purely pictorial or musical or poetic potentials in freedom from the dominance of either natural or utilitarian kinds of lawfulness. Color in a natural being serves a subordinate function, since the specific nature of the being is dominant. Color in a useful artifact serves a subordinate function, usually decorative. Color in a painting serves a definitory function as one of the essential painterly materials or means, actualized according to purely pictorial compositional lawfulness. Works of art are therefore a distinctive domain of beings standing under their own artistic lawfulness, free from subservience to any other. And their link with human life is that only human beings can bring them into being. The artistic autonomy of the works links up with the artistic autonomy of makers and recipients in the sense that the human beings, too, are liberated from subservience to, and concern with, any other overriding kind of natural or utilitarian lawfulness. The actualization of the purely artistic inner potentiality of the works corresponds to the actualization of a disinterested human potentiality for service to these works. Artistic freedom is service to artistic lawfulness. As the works enrich the world, so their creation and reception enrich human life. This does account for the fact that our engagement with art differs from our engagement with nature and with useful artifacts.

Kandinsky's comprehensive theory can preserve all three functions. The key lies in his giving the distinctive materials or means of each species of art definitory significance. A significant link of art with human life does not depend on Aristotle's *mimesis* 2, nor on any high-brow or low-brow utilitarianism, whether that be didactic, hedonistic, therapeutic, expressive, impressive, formulative, symbolic, revelatory, or *Rezeptionsästhetik*. Art is not some alien content dressed up in decorative garb, but an intrinsic artistic content in its own compositional form.

To answer the systematic question: since all three functions can be preserved at a comprehensive level that encompasses both representational and nonrepresentational works, Aristotle's theory, which lacks such comprehensiveness, must be judged to be dated. It cannot fulfill one of the crucial desiderata of modern and contemporary theory of art. Paradoxically, Kandinsky achieves his theoretical solution by what looks like a very Aristotelian move: giving the distinctive artistic materials or means constitutive and definitory significance. Aristotle himself, though he recognized the material cause as constitutive, lodged the definitory descriptive content of an *ousia* in its formal-final cause, which therefore was prior to the material cause. It may well be this priority, which bars him from a theory of art that is not constitutively and definitorily focused on representational content.

But as a final evaluation, the fact that his theory is dated in one respect should not obscure its enduring significance in other respects. Chief among these is his recognition that a work of art needs an intrinsic compositional principle, which must be art-specific. It must give a work a distinctively artistic constitutive structure and qualitative descriptive content. For structure without content is formalistic, while content without structure is chaotic. Some of the most interesting debates in theory of art concern the possibility that the role of compositional principle may be played by different factors. For example: we might consider a merely episodic structure in a tragedy most tragic of all, while Aristotle considers it least tragic of all. He takes the action as compositional principle, one might also consider lack of action as playing that role. One might take meter as compositional principle in poetry, iteration of themes in a novel, or three-dimensionality in sculpture. For us, there is great theoretical and practical flexibility against the shared background of the recognition that something must function as compositional principle. It is Aristotle who provided that shared background and thereby won the debate with Plato. It would be quaint for any theoretician today to conceptualize a painting of a man as a *man* rather than as a *painting*. In *Poetics* 18, Aristotle seems to suggest that different factors in a tragedy might play the role of compositional principle, giving rise to complex, pathetic, ethical, or simple works. But in characteristic fashion, he gives paradigmatic standing to only one, the complex.

With Aristotle's recognition of the need for a compositional principle went the recognition of the need for art-specific standards of rightness and excellence (*orthotes* and *he kata ten technen kalliste tragodia*). He thereby achieved some of the perennial desiderata of any theory of art: to account for the integral being of works of art; to resist *hetero-telic* definitions; to resist reduction of the art-specific to what is not art-specific; to distinguish what is essential and definitory from what is not; to resist obscurantism; to account for our distinctive engagement with art. And finally, to extend Ockham's Razor: like entities, senses are not to be multiplied beyond necessity. Aristotle's theory does without postulating a special aesthetic sense, a conceptual and ontological economy worthy of emulation.

APPENDIX: TEXTUAL EVIDENCE

The question what is to count as textual evidence and what as counter-evidence is complicated by the fact that a number of Aristotle's key terms are ambiguous and so could be taken either way. They can be taken as having either an intrinsic or an extrinsic reference. If taken intrinsically, they could refer either to the action (object-centering) or to the protagonist (agent-centering) of the tragedy. If taken extrinsically, they refer to the audience (patient-centering). All three modes of centering could therefore be, and indeed have been, ascribed to some of the same terms. The occurrence of such a term is thus in itself neither evidence nor counterevidence. What makes it so is its context, both direct and indirect. As Nehamas notes: "Gould's discussion shows that the words themselves seldom settle the issue of what—an event or an experience—is being referred to in the text . . . understanding of each of their occurrences in context is crucial.[1]

Context is many-faceted both in its direct and indirect aspects. Direct aspects comprise such things as location in the *Poetics*. The evidential weight to be placed on a term is greater if it occurs in the wording or explication of the formal definition of a tragedy than if it occurs in a less crucial place. It is greater if it occurs as part of the argument or in the resolution of *aporiai* than if it occurs as part of the subsequent *(eita, pros toutois, semeion)* empirical confirmation of the argument. Other direct aspects are, e.g., the technical use of terms, which lends them greater precision and weight than nontechnical or colloquial use; the polemical use of terms, when Aristotle sets his own understanding off against the mistaken beliefs *(hamartemata)* of others, often citing Homer as his ally; the use of terms in explicit mutually exclusive contrasts such as "in its own right" versus "in relation to" *(kath hauten* versus *pros ti)* or "focused on one person" versus "focused on one action" *(peri hena* versus *peri mian praxin)*, which gives them both sharpness and authority, since contrastive thinking is an Aristotelian hallmark.

Indirect aspects comprise such intangibles as the mood or tone of the text, since the evidential weight of terms is affected by whether Aristotle is prescriptive (*dei, chre, ananke*, etc.), argumentative (*epei, ara*, etc.), didactic, polemical, ironic, or tentative. But more importantly, they comprise all the implications of the terms as they occur in their direct contexts. It is these implications that link the *Poetics* with Aristotle's philosophy as a whole. Unless textual evidence to the contrary is present, these implications should be the normal Aristotelian ones. This seems *prima facie* demanded by one's taking the *Poetics* to be an Aristotelian treatise. The principle of charity demands that these Aristotelian implications be held to be consistent throughout the *Poetics* and indeed the *corpus,* barring textual counterevidence. In the case of Aristotle, an unusually consistent and systematic thinker, the principle of charity is a fundamental exegetical device.

It is this device that underlies the approach of the present study. I have argued that the *Poetics* is Aristotelian in the sense that it is philosophy of being in terms of his distinctive understanding of being. I have therefore taken the terminology of the *Poetics* in the context of that understanding, by gradual adumbration of its subject matter and by letting the technical terms carry their normal Aristotelian implications.

This approach makes the *Poetics* appear consistent, technical, and well structured as well as integrated into the whole of Aristotelian philosophy. It also makes it appear radical (e.g., *vis-à-vis* Plato), innovative, and very subtle, but also in some respects dated. What is to me the most surprising discovery is the pivotal importance of the "focused on one person/focused on one action" (*peri hena/peri mian praxin*) contrast of *Poetics* 8, well expressed by Cooper: "The plot is that synthesis of incidents which gives form or being to the play as a whole."[2]

My approach makes the *Poetics* appear in a certain way, and that may well be the problem with it. For any approach, mine or any other, may be something of a self-fulfilling prophecy. Given the ambiguity of some of the key terms, what counts as textual evidence can also be taken as counterevidence.

Take *katharsis* as an example. It can be taken, and has indeed been taken, in all three modes of centering: as the *katharsis* of the action intrinsic to the tragedy, as that of the agent intrinsic to the tragedy (the protagonist), as that of the patient extrinsic to the tragedy (the audience). Depending on the mode of centering, a tragedy appears as very different sorts of things.

When *katharsis* is taken as object-centered, a tragedy appears as a substantial composite being (*synolon*) intrinsically focused on its action as its compositional principle, its "principle which functions as its soul" (*arche hoion psyche*). Else has emphasized this structural-compositional focus: "Thus the poet's work . . . is to be measured above all *structurally* . . . a poetic structure of events, something that is objective, measurable, potentially common to other works."[3] And Halliwell has stressed its objective priority to audience reaction: "directed more towards the objective presentation than the subjective reception . . . more towards their intrinsic validity, in terms of necessity or probability, than their capacity to convince an audience . . . Aristotle's general reluctance to appeal to the mentality of audiences as a standard of poetic practice."[4]

When *katharsis* is taken as agent-centered, a tragedy appears as a religious rite, a ritual of purification, e.g., "We may see the *catharsis* which takes place in the theatre as kin to those rituals of purification which effect atonement for agents . . . the occasion both of Oedipus' staged purification and of the audience's sympathetic purification."[5]

When *katharsis* is taken as patient-centered, a tragedy appears as an analogue of rhetorical speechmaking or medical treatment: "[T]here is for Aristotle an . . . analogy between poetry and rhetoric. . . . Just as the orator constructs arguments with a view to what his audience will understand and be prepared to believe, so the playwright must order the material of his plot-structure in such a way as to convince his audience of its intelligibility."[6] If the didactic aspect is stressed, "the theater [is] regarded almost as a form of adult education."[7]

The ambiguity that attaches to *katharsis* also attaches to other terms that may have an intrinsic as well as an extrinsic reference, e.g., "persuasive" *(pithanon)*, "likely" *(eikos)*, "generally" *(katholou)*, "work" *(ergon)*, "human" *(anthropinon)*, "pitiful" *(eleeinon)*, "fearsome" *(phoberon)*, "end" *(telos)*, "affliction" *(pathos)*, as Halliwell has recognized: "point of reference: if the focus is on an audience . . . subjective sense of probability . . . if on the inherent relations . . . objective sense."[8] But if one distinguishes between their lexical and their textual meaning (i.e., their meaning in isolation and their meaning in their direct and indirect textual context), most arguments may be solvable.

To that end, I make a few suggestions as to translation.

a. Technical terms should be translated technically, not colloquially. Otherwise translation obscures the terminological formality and precision of the text. E.g., "differentia" *(diaphora)* is mostly used technically by Aristotle, as definitory differentia, and should be so translated. Only when he uses it colloquially should one use a different term in the translation.

b. The same term when used in the same sense should be translated by the same term. Otherwise translation obscures the terminological consistency and continuity of the text. E.g., when *diaphora* is used technically, it should be translated by the same word throughout, not sometimes by "distinction" and sometimes by "difference." And *mimesis* 2 should not sometimes be translated by "imitation" and sometimes by "enactment."

c. Translation should preserve a term's level of generality. E.g., the tragedy-animal analogy implies *mimesis* 1, not *mimesis* 2.

d. Textual and exegetical arguments for text establishment and translation should be indicated as such, since they differ in evidentiary weight.

e. Translation should orient itself by the three modes of centering, since the meaning of terms depends on their categorization. E.g., objective or subjective translation depends on the mode of centering, on where the definitory *telos* is located.

What militates against these principles of translation is largely our wish to make our rendering of the text readable and stylistically appealing. That is aided by the use of colloquial terms and by the avoidance of repetition of the same term. Aristotle was not much concerned with such considerations, and perhaps here, too, *Aristoteles ex Aristotele* needs to be the heuristic principle in order to make exegetical disagreements amenable to resolution by providing a common terminological ground.

     The present study has approached the *Poetics* contextually and taken its terms as primarily object-centered. Its prime objective has been to work out the Aristotelian implications of this approach. It would be interesting to see the Aristotelian implications of an agent-centered and of a patient-centered approach worked out as well. Only then would a truly perspicacious metalevel debate be possible. But a final application of the principle of charity may be in order: an approach that can resolve problems generated by other approaches may thereby be to some extent confirmed as being closest to Aristotle. The present approach seems able to resolve at least some exegetical problems.

     I select four such problems. The first concerns the relationship of the *Poetics* to Aristotle's philosophy as a whole. The second and third concern the relationship of different aspects of the *Poetics* to each other. The fourth concerns the relationship of the *Poetics* to ourselves.

     The first is formulated by Butcher: "There is here a formal contradiction from which there appears to be no escape. It would seem that Aristotle in generalizing from the observed effects of works of art raises the subjective side of fine art into a prominence which is hardly in keeping with his whole philosophical system."[9] It seems more likely that Butcher's idealizing exegesis is wrong than that Aristotle's theory is "hardly in keeping with his whole philosophical system." The present approach resolves this "formal contradiction" by showing the *Poetics* to be well integrated into Aristotle's "whole philosophical system." It does so by specifying the pervasive substantive-methodological conceptual constants of that system and showing how they are present in the *Poetics*. Frede notes Aristotle's "tendency to import the same principles in all disciplines . . . these principles in fact allow for quite some flexibility." She, too, sees his "ontological system" as basic to his *Poetics*.[10]

The second exegetical problem is formulated by Nussbaum as an inconsistency in the text. "In *Poetics* 13 . . . Aristotle remarks: 'first, it is clear that good men *[epieikeis andras]* should not be shown changing from good to bad fortune—for this is not pitiable or fearful, but disgusting *[miaron]*'." She sees this as conflicting with "a great deal of evidence in the *Poetics* and other works." Her exegesis creates this inconsistency because she sees the definitory *telos* of a tragedy as "the generation of tragic responses" in an audience, namely, the generation of pity and fear. She holds that "the ethically controversial material of pity and fear is not a kernel of content inside the tragic form; it forms the form, and the plots that are its 'starting point and soul' (50 a 38–39). It informs the choice of the hero, the type of story chosen, and the causal structure linking the events. We can add that it also shapes two further features of tragic plot in which Aristotle shows a particular interest: reversal *(peripeteia)* and recognition *(anagnorisis)*."[11] Her patient-centered exegesis of *Poetics* 13, 1452b34–36 is indeed inconsistent with "a great deal of evidence in the *Poetics* and other works." For it contradicts *Poetics* 6, which declares *mythos*, the structure of the action *(systasis pragmaton)*, to be the principle and soul of a tragedy. A tragedy cannot have two different principles that function as its souls *(archai hoion psychai)*. And the text clearly first elucidates the structure of the action, then makes the pitiful and fearsome an objective "kernel of content inside the tragic form," then matches *ethe* to this structure. The present approach solves this exegetical problem by showing that *Poetics* 13.1452b34–36 treats *ethe* as secondary and incorporates the pitiful and fearsome into the structure of the action as its objective emotive content. The emotive content is not prior to that structure, and the response of an audience is not prior to anything but rather derivative from the tragedy *(apo tes tragodias)*. The alleged inconsistency vanishes.

The third exegetical problem is found in, but not acknowledged as a problem by, Halliwell. On the one hand, he understands that the *Poetics* rejects an agent-centered structure as a mistake and instead demands that a tragedy be structured around one action. On the other hand, he speaks of "the larger agent-centered view of drama which the treatise consistently offers."[12] Clearly, the *Poetics* could not advocate both without inconsistency. A tragedy could no more be structured around two different things (an agent and an action) than it could have two different souls or two different definitory *tele*. The present approach solves this exegetical problem by showing that the compositional primacy of the action and the consequent secondary status of *ethe* are held to consistently throughout the text.

The fourth exegetical problem is Lear's contention that the *Poetics* is dated in a damaging sense: "It might seem odd to a modern reader to see Aristotle *define* tragedy in terms of its effect, for in a modern climate we tend to think that a work of art should be definable in its own terms, independently of whatever effect it might have on its audience. But it would be anachronistic to insist that Aristotle could not have been defining tragedy in terms of its effect on the audience. Poetry *(poiesis),* for Aristotle, is a type of making *(poiesis),* and the activity of any making occurs *in* the person or thing towards which the making is directed. For example, the activity of the teacher teaching is occurring, not in the teacher, but in the students who are learning; the activity of the builder building is occurring, not in the builder, but in the house being built. It stands to reason that, for Aristotle, the activity of the poet creating his tragedy occurs ultimately in an audience actively appreciating a performance of the play."[13] Though the present approach admits that Aristotle's theory of art is dated in some respects, it solves Lear's exegetical problem by showing that it is not dated in a damaging sense. For it is precisely the sharpness and clarity of Aristotle's categorial distinction between *ousia* and *pros ti,* between what a tragedy is in its own nature *(kath hauten, kata tes hautes physin)* and in relation to an audience *(pros ta theatra),* that makes the *Poetics* deeply relevant to "a modern climate."[14]

A poet is not a teacher, and a tragedy is not a teaching aid. A poet is not a *rhetor,* and a tragedy is not a rhetorical means of persuasion. A poet is not a doctor, and a tragedy is neither a homeopathic nor an allopathic course of treatment. A poet is not a priest, and a tragedy is not a ritual of purification. A poet is a maker, and the product of his making is a tragedy, a *tragike mimesis.*

NOTES

Preface

1. Ross 1966 (originally published 1924); Kassel 1965; Lucas 1968; Halliwell 1987. Janko 1987, xxii, also bases his translation on Kassel's text "which is the standard one in use." But he records more disagreements, mostly because he believes that Kassel has not given enough weight to MS B and the Arabic "whose importance has only been demonstrated relatively recently." He also uses Hellenistic sources, but given their general rhetorical bias, they may not be of much help in understanding the *Poetics*. I have found no textual disagreements that impact the argument.

Heath 1996, LXV: "The edition I have worked from is R. Kassel's Oxford Classical Text . . . I have frequently departed from the readings printed by Kassel." But I have found no crucial departures.

Introduction

1. There is an interesting parallel to my project. Much of a recent volume on Aristotle's *Ethics* (Sim, ed. 1995) is devoted to exploring whether and in what sense the *Ethics* should be read in light of the *Metaphysics*. Different contributors reach different conclusions.

Chapter 1. Approach to the Corpus as a Whole

1. For some discussion of approaches, see Düring and Owen, eds. 1960, particularly the essays by Ross, Owen, and de Vogel.

I am in agreement with Gill 1989, 9: "First, I assume that Aristotle's treatises can be read as a coherent whole. Thus I differ from many interpreters who think that Aristotle's writings reflect his intellectual development." Reeve 2000, xv, puts it picturesquely: "[D]evelopmental hypotheses largely piggyback on interpretive ones."

2. Scholars differ concerning the features of Aristotelian method. Cleary 1988, 74f., denies that an Aristotelian *episteme* has a distinctive method at all: "Aristotle's tendency to differentiate the sciences according to their characteristic objects rather than by their respective methods." But this position is not widely shared.

McKeon (Olson 1965, 208), traces differences in method to differences in the different aspects of things: "As applied to the arts, the accomplishment of Aristotle's philosophic method was the separation of problems involved in the mode of existence of an object produced or of a productive power (which might properly be treated in physics and metaphysics) as well as problems involved in the effects of artificial objects or artistic efforts (as treated in psychology, morals, and politics) or in doctrinal cogency and emotional persuasiveness (as treated in logic and rhetoric) from problems which bear on the traits of an artistic construction consequent simply on its being a work of art."

See Owens (Catan 1981, 1–13) and Gilson 1965, 123, on the ontological and cognitive priority of the object to the subject. This is applied to the *Poetics* by Else 1957, 403 f. For a dissenting view, see Nussbaum 1986. But against this see Wians (Preus and Anton 1992). See also Aristotle's *Categories* VII.7b23–24 and XII.14b10–24.

3. The *Metaphysics* is more general and foundational than the *Posterior Analytics*, because it lays down the basic philosophical conceptualization of all things, while the latter is more particularly concerned with the foundations of demonstrative science. I use the term *categories*, based on the *Metaphysics' kategoriai tou ontos*, rather than the term *predicates*. For the distinction between them in Aristotle's *Categories*, see Anton 1993.

4. Düring and Owen 1960, 163–190. Owen coined the phrase "focal meaning" to indicate that the meaning of attributes in the secondary categories derives from the primary substance whose attributes they are.

5. One notable exception was discovered by Owen 1960, see chapter 3, Note 1.

6. I have argued for the nonreductive nature of the *pros hen*. Husain 1981, 208–218. The Oxford translation does not take sufficient account of this and links the two questions by a misleadingly reductive "just." For this there is no textual basis, since the *touto* that links them in the text only supplies a grammatical reference without reductive import. And the proliferation of modifying expressions, "chiefly" *(malista)*, "primarily" *(proton)*, and "so to say exclusively" *(monon hos eipein)*, emphasizes the nonreductive nature of the reformulation. For *malista* as a superlative implies a relation to a comparative and positive; *proton* implies a contrast with something secondary *(proteron* in contrast to *hysteron, haplos* in contrast to *pos, proton* in contrast to *eita)*; and the *hos eipein*, which modifies *monon*, takes any reductive sting out of it.

7. Code 1984, has convincingly argued for the largely *aporetic* nature of much of *Met*. VII. But I see no reason not to accept the plain language of the text in *Met*. IX. 7, unlike Gill 1989, chapter 5, who argues that it does not extend *paronymy* to the material cause of artifacts, 161: "One should have qualms about the treatment of artifacts in *Metaphysics* IX 7 . . . plausible for contexts of chemical combination . . . implausible for many contexts of artificial production."

8. Owens has most emphatically argued for the identity in the descriptive content of perceptible and intelligible forms in things and in the knower's soul (Catan 1981, 74–80).

Sparshott 1994, 134, speaks of "Aristotle's sturdily realistic view of the world," meaning epistemological realism.

Chapter 2. Approach to the Poetics

1. An argument from the silence of primary and/or secondary literature is never conclusive. But since the *Poetics* as an Aristotelian treatise is *prima facie* to be read in the light of his general philosophy, some argument and textual support would seem to be needed if someone were to hold that it falls outside his distinctive understanding of being.

2. Some scholars see the *Poetics* as having a distinctive subject matter of its own, others do not. Aristotle's own strongest argument for the independence of his theory of art occurs in *Poetics* 25, which holds that the standards of rightness *(orthotes)* of art are different from those of any other *techne*.

McKeon (Crane1952, 164 f.): "Aristotle is engaged in making literary distinctions, within the field of imitative art . . . his criteria are derived from a restricted field of discussion without reference beyond. . . . These primary distinctions serve a function in Aristotle's analysis comparable to that of the first principles of a science. . . . [These are] fundamental distinctions derived from the subject matter with which the inquiry is concerned, and they supply the apparatus about which the analysis of poetry is organized . . . in virtue of this method, whatever pertains to the subject of a particular science is reserved for treatment in that science." According to McKeon, *Politics* VIII.7 is not relevant to the *Poetics*, since it deals with art from the perspective of its political uses.

3. Scholars have recognized the *Poetics* as being a metalevel *epistemic* investigation of poetical *techne*. See Halliwell 1987, 3: "The major concern of the work . . . is theoretical: that is to say, it bears systematically and prescriptively on the intrinsic nature of poetry." And Rorty 1992, 3: "the *Poetics* . . . a philosophical study intended to analyse the structures and functions of the range of poetic genres as if they were biological species." Also Grube 1958, xiii; Crane 1953, 65; Heath 1996, xi.

4. Aristotle uses terms such as *to gignomenon* and *to ergon* to designate the product of a *techne* or *poiesis*. A tragedy is such a product, it is not a *praxis*. Yet some scholars have so characterized it, while others have not.

The most emphatic statement that the *Poetics* is about the *praxis* of writing a tragedy rather than about the tragedy itself as the separate product of that writing comes from Else 1957, 279: "[T]he six parts are not thought of by Aristotle primarily as parts of the product (the play), but as constituent elements . . . moments in the activity of building a tragedy."

By contrast, Crane 1953, 54: "[Aristotle is] concentrating on the poetic product as distinguished from the process of its composition;" 88: "[W]hat are called epics, tragedies, comedies, etc. appear to constitute a distinctive class of things."

5. Gill 1989, chapter 5, uses the criterion of "vertical unity" to distinguish between substantial and nonsubstantial artifacts, so that some artifacts are *ousiai* while others are not.

Katayama 1999, uses the criteria of "eternity," actuality, and separation to deny substantial status to all artifacts, but he does not consider Aristotle's other criteria of substantiality: being a real and hence predicative subject of accidental attributes, potentialities, and changes; being a *syntheton* constituted by form and matter; being a separable this.

One fairly frequently held position, that works of art are accidents inhering in nonartistic substances, namely, their matter, would seem to make no sense in the case of a tragedy. Ross 1966, cxxii: "Now artistic production is never the production of a new substance but only of a new shape, etc., in an existing substance." Cf. Kosman (Gotthelf and Lennox 1987, 387 f.).

By contrast, Gilson 1965, 104: "Each and every one of the artist's works is an enrichment of the sum total of substantial being."

6. Butcher 1951, 116 f: "'Art imitates nature' . . . was never intended to differentiate between fine and useful art. . . . In the *Physics* (ii.2.194 a 21) the point of the comparison is that alike in art and in nature there is the union of matter (ὕλη) with constitutive form (εἶδος) . . . art in general imitates the method of nature."

Woodruff (Rorty 1992, 78): "[A] profession *(techne)* like medicine or architecture works like nature in that both *techne* and nature subordinate their products teleologically, for the sake of ends (194 a 21); and this relation between *techne* and nature he describes as mimesis. . . . Mimesis here has nothing to do with imitation or representation; it produces health, rather than a simulacrum of health."

Halliwell 1986, 50f: "*Techne* represents the first layer or level in Aristotle's concept of the mimetic arts . . . Aristotle's acceptance of the framework of *techne* for the interpretation of poetry . . . imports an inescapably objectivist element, as well as a naturalistic teleology . . . the mimetic artist is devoted to the realization of aims which are determined independently of him . . . by the objective principles."

7. McKeon (Crane 1952, 161). 166: "The Platonic and the Aristotelian approaches to . . . art . . . are mutually incommensurable." Cf. Halliwell 1986, 21 f.

8. Scholars have recognized that art is *mimetic*, while *logos* is not. Cf. Halliwell 1987, 172: "Ar. needed to clear a distinctive 'space' for poetry outside the sphere of directly affirmative and truth-seeking discourses such as history, philosophy and science." Halliwell 1986, 55, speaks of such truth-seeking *logoi* as "non-mimetic ways," in which universals can be communicated.

Else 1957, 491: "This idea, that the poet lurks behind and in his characters, speaking through them to establish an emotional sway over his audience . . . runs counter to . . . Aristotle's theory of poetry, and particularly of tragedy, which was built on the premise that the characters speak *instead* of the poet." Cf. Crane 1953, 86.

9. Sim (Sim 1995, xii): "This final end is the good of the thing, or the form-as-its-good; it is the essential nature of the thing acting *as* a value."

10. Gilson 1965. But Gilson is clear that for Aristotle, "Calology occupies a very small place in his meditations" (71). Cf. Butcher 1951, 161: "Some critics . . .

have attempted to show that the fundamental principles of fine art are deduced by Aristotle from the idea of the beautiful. But this is to antedate the theory of modern aesthetics, and to read into Aristotle more than any impartial interpretation can find in him . . . Aristotle's conception of fine art . . . is entirely detached from any theory of the beautiful." 241: "From this definition it appears first, that the *genus* of tragedy is Imitation. This it has in common with all the fine arts."

11. I have argued elsewhere that these three are related, Husain 1992, 64–73. My reflections were spurred by an expression I owe to Kenneth Schmitz of the University of Toronto: "An *ousia* is a being with a recursive center." Cf. Sparshott 1982, 28 f: "The position . . . in which the values of art are held strictly separate from those of life as a whole, is Aristotle's. It is not Plato's."

12. Furth (Mourelatos 1974, 241–270).

13. Anton (Georgopoulos 1993, 34). Cf. Halliwell 1986, 319.

14. ἐπεὶ δ᾽ ἐστὶ τῶν μὲν ἔσχατον ἡ χρῆσις (οἷον ὄψεως ἡ ὅρασις, καὶ οὐθὲν γίγνεται παρὰ ταύτην ἕτερον ἀπὸ τῆς ὄψεως), ἀπ᾽ ἐνίων δὲ γίγνεταί τι (οἷον ἀπὸ τῆς οἰκοδομικῆς οἰκία παρὰ τὴν οἰκοδόμησιν), ὅμως οὐθὲν ἧττον ἔνθα μὲν τέλος, ἔνθα δὲ μᾶλλον τέλος τῆς δυνάμεώς ἐστιν· ἡ γὰρ οἰκοδόμησις ἐν τῷ οἰκοδομουμένῳ, καὶ ἅμα γίγνεται καὶ ἔστι τῇ οἰκίᾳ. ὅσων μὲν οὖν ἕτερον τί ἐστι παρὰ τὴν χρῆσιν τὸ γιγνόμενον, τούτων μὲν ἡ ἐνέργεια ἐν τῷ ποιουμένῳ ἐστίν (οἷον ἥ τε οἰκοδόμησις ἐν τῷ οἰκοδομουμένῳ καὶ ἡ ὕφανσις ἐν τῷ ὑφαινομένῳ, ὁμοίως δὲ καὶ ἐπὶ τῶν ἄλλων; *Met.* IX. 1050a23–33.

15. Georgiadis 1978, 58 f: "[I]n contrast to autotelic activities, the very *raison d'être* of making is the production of an external thing. . . . Thus, from an ontological point of view, the products of making belong to the realm of material, contingent things . . . which, once produced, have an independent status and characteristics of their own." Cf. Crane 1953, 43: "Poetics . . . the good it aims at is not to be found in the activities . . . but rather in products . . . [which] have values in themselves which are independent of the character and motives of the agents who brought them into being."

16. Hartmann 1966, 470, sets out a *Rezeptionsästhetik* that is the antithesis of Aristotle's theory of art: "das zeitlich lückenhafte Existieren von Kunstwerken: bald sind sie von der Erde verschwunden und nur noch die dinglich—realen 'Vordergründe' drücken sich in Museen und Bibliotheken herum, bald sind sie wieder da . . . alles je nachdem, ob der adäquat aufnehmende Geist vorhanden ist oder nicht."

17. A sampling of other approaches that link the *Poetics* with other texts: Grube 1958, xvii: "The *Poetics* must be read with the . . . *Politics* in mind." xxvii: "[T]aken together, the *Poetics* and . . . *Rhetoric* . . . contain the essential thought on poetry and literature." Kosman (Rorty 1992, 68): "*Poetics* . . . sequel to the *Ethics* and *Politics*." Else 1957, 73: "[B]ecause poetry is a portrayal of the life of action the closest affinities with the *Poetics* will turn up in the other works that deal with the 'practical' sphere: the *Rhetoric*, the *Politics*, and especially the *Ethics*."

Chapter 3.   Levels within the Poetics

1. Düring and Owen 1960, 166. Since the rubbing of one's eyes refers specifically to the absence of Aristotle's distinctive understanding of being in *E.E.* I. 8, which results in an *aporia* elsewhere resolved in terms of that understanding, some such rubbing would have to be occasioned by the *Poetics* if one wanted to argue that the first level is not implicitly present.

2. Halliwell 1987, 69.

3. The two liberties most widely noted and criticized are Aristotle's neglect of the lyrical component and of the divine in Greek tragedies. Cf. Else 1957, 554: "Nowhere is his blindness to the real *raison d'être* of the chorus in Greek tragedy more dreadfully apparent than here." Also Halliwell 1986, 148: "[T]he world in which such heroes belonged was one in which powers other than those of human agency were a major source of suffering and tragedy. It is this latter fact for which Aristotle's theory of the genre does not make full provision, and it is in this respect that theory and practice are no longer in harmony . . . the work's neglect of the religious element in Greek tragedy." Cf. 34, 248 ff.

4. Lucas 1968, 82. Halliwell 1987, 84: "Ar.'s teleological emphasis: it is the eventual, perfectly developed form which matters, not the first stage in the growth towards it." Also Halliwell 1986, 49: "[T]he history of tragedy has to be comprehended ultimately in terms not of contingent human choices and tradition, but of natural teleology mediated through . . . human discovery of what was there to be found."

5. The backward reference is to chapters 1–3, not to 4–5 as Else takes it. Lucas 1968, 96: "E. [Else] explains γινόμενον as imperf., repeating the ἐγίγνετο of 49 a 13 and referring to the way in which tragedy realized its own nature while developing in time, τῶν εἰρημένων being taken as the historical sketch in Ch. 4. This is not readily intelligible."

6. The causal language of chapters 1–3 is obscured by translating *en hois* as "media," since the *en* is not local but indicates the material cause, a quite common Aristotelian technical locution. "Media" anachronistically suggests communication, not constitutive material causality. Aristotle uses the *en* to indicate both material and formal causality, e.g., *Met.* VIII. 1043a34–35; IX. 1050a15–16. McKeon 1946, 193: "Language . . . constitutes the natural means of imitation in the arts of literature and the matter of which literary works are formed."

7. There are no textual disagreements that seriously bear on the argument, and both Else and Halliwell have recognized that the text, particularly in its main chapters on plot, is a coherent argument and much less obscure and difficult than is often alleged. See Else 1957, vii and Halliwell 1986, 33–37.

8. Translations of this definition differ dramatically, the most fundamental differences focusing on *katharsis* and its categorization (whether it is in the category of *ousia* or of *pros ti*), from which the categorization of a tragedy as a whole follows. If *katharsis* refers intrinsically to the tragedy and so is in the category of *ousia*, a tragedy is a substantial being analogous to a living animal. If it refers extrinsically to the audience and so is in the category of *pros ti*, a tragedy is an

accidental being analogous to medical treatment or rhetorical speechmaking. My translation opts for the former.

Part of my textual reason is that "achieving" *(perainousa)*, whose direct accusative object *katharsin* is, does not normally denote transeunt efficient causality in the category of *pros ti* for Aristotle. He would normally use "produce" *(poiei)* for this (e.g., *Poetics* 26.1462a11–12). *Perainousa*, which contains "limit" *(peras)*, is not normally a synonym for *poiein* and is translated much more naturally as "achieving a limitation or completion." This means that *katharsis* is the achievement of an intrinsic self-limitation or completion in a tragedy, of the unity and wholeness of its action, by making its sequential-causal structure clear *(katharon)*.

Such achievement may succeed more or less, so that *mimesis* 2 may be more or less *tragike*, and Aristotle uses *tragikon* in the positive, the comparative, and the superlative. Taking *perainousa katharsin* as intrinsic, gives a good grounding for this use. It has been winning the assent of more scholars, e.g., Anton (Georgopoulos 1993, 26 ff.): "Tragedy, then, is an imitation *[mimesis]* of an action, important and complete, and of a certain magnitude, by means of language embellished, and with ornaments used separately for each part, about human beings in action, not in narrative; carrying to completion, through a course of events involving pity *(eleos)* and fear *(phobos)*, the purification of those painful or fatal acts which have that quality... what is being brought to an end in tragedy is not the catharsis of emotions *(pathe)* but the clarification of the incidents that comprise the plot, the *mythos* ... the completion of *mythos* and not the purgation of emotions is the purpose of a tragedy. As for the benefits of tragedy, the *oikeia hedone* and the *didaskalia* it offers, they call for a separate study." Else 1957, 439 ff., is in agreement with Anton. But for a dissenting view, see Janko (Rorty 1992, 346), Gould 1990, 49 and Note 2, and Belfiore 1992, 58 ff.

9. The *pases tes tragodias* can be translated either as "every tragedy" or "tragedy in general," but this does not affect the argument nor the prescriptive force of the text here. Aristotle's elucidation of the dative *logoi* as "language with rhythm and melody" makes it intrinsic and constitutive, the material of tragedy. And *lexis* as "the composition of spoken meters" is equally intrinsic. While *logos* and *lexis* can mean "delivery" and are then linked with the *rhetor's* or rhapsode's or actor's *techne*, this is clearly not their meaning here.

10. Halliwell 1986, 141 f: "[T]he *Poetics* contains an original development of the word *praxis* to mean the organized totality of a play's structure of events, its complete dramatic framework.... This new piece of poetic and dramatic vocabulary also represents a new concept ... refined by Aristotle to the status of a technical term ... 'action' *(praxis)* is the structure of a play's events viewed as a dimension of the events themselves ... the design or significant organization of the work of art ... the plot-structure." 144: "[U]nity is the principal property of the *mythos*. ... Unity arises out of the causal and consequential relations ... and it is the connective sequence of these events which constitutes the intelligible structure that Aristotle terms both the action and the plot-structure."

11. Halliwell 1987, Commentary on chapter 6. Else 1957, 253 and 529, calls it "an obsession" and a "fixation," and Butcher 1951, 332 and 343 f., calls it an "exaggeration."

12. Aristotle uses emotive terms in noun-form or in adjectival form inter-changeably, though the adjectival form predominates. I translate all of them objectively, as characterizing the action, the *praxis phthartike kai odynera* of the tragedy. Other emotive terms, also translated objectively, are: *deinon, oiktron, philanthropon.*

Commentators translate them partly objectively (as characterizing the ac-tion) and partly subjectively (as characterizing the audience), though the objec-tive translation is gaining ground. Anton (Georgopoulos 1993, 6): "*pathemata* means events, doing, incidents. In the context of the definition of tragedy the word refers to the quality and type of events proper to tragic poetry: pitiful (*eleeina*) and terrible (*phobera*). . . . The emotionally charged incidents, *pathemata*, as con-stituent elements of a tragic plot or *mythos*." Cf. Heath 1996, xxi.

Else 1957, 328 f: "[T]ragedy is an imitation of fearful and pitiable events . . . its special emotional content. . . . The premise that tragedy is to imitate 'not only a complete action but fearful and pitiable events' is drawn from the definition in chapter 6 in its expanded form . . . here we find the concept of the μίμησις φοβερῶν καὶ ἐλεεινῶν taken as the premise for a whole section of Aristotle's work, and a section which must be regarded as primary . . . since Aristotle is talking about events, structural elements in the play, fearful and pathetic happenings are most effectively brought about—when they come about unexpectedly but logically (δι' ἄλληλα). This is one of the most pregnant remarks in the entire *Poetics*. It is in fact the key not only to Aristotle's conception of the complex plot but to his doctrine of *hamartia* and *catharsis*." The same point is argued persuasively by Nehamas (Rorty 1992, 306 f.). For a dissenting view, see Belfiore 1992, chapter 8.

13. Race (unpublished manuscript, 4), has contrasted Pindar and Aristotle on *aitia:* "The major difference is that Pindar ascribes the αἴτια to the inscrutable designs of the gods, whereas for Aristotle the αἴτια are rational causes. Pindar's view is essentially religious; Aristotle's is fundamentally philosophical." I believe that it would be congruent with his view to say that for Aristotle, the *aitia* of the tragic action are *kathara*, which implies that *katharsis* in the definition of tragedy refers to the action.

14. The difference between Aristotle's and our understanding of "functional" in theory of art must be kept in mind, if confusion is to be avoided. For only immanent constitutive causal functioning is definitory for an *ousia*, while no transeunt efficient causal effect is. The term "work" (*ergon*) can express both, and only the context can make clear which is intended. The mere fact that *ergon* appears in a text does not mean that transeunt efficient causality is meant. The intrinsic *ergon* of the plot is to give unity to the tragedy, to "besoul" or enform it, cf. Booth (Rorty 1992, 407, Note 21). Sparshott 1994, 341: "When Aristotle thinks in terms of function, he does so primarily in terms of the internal function-ing of a system, how it works."

The modern understanding of "functional," by contrast, is what Aristotle would call transeunt efficient causality. Smith (Preus and Anton 1992, 294): "Func-tional definitions define things in terms of their causal roles. . . . Borrowing from recent philosophy of mind, we may say that a functional definition of a thing defines it as a causal role: to give a functional definition of F is to specify causal relationships to other things." Belfiore 1992, 3: "[T]he plot has the function *(ergon)* of arousing the emotions of pity and fear, and of producing pleasure and katharsis by this means." Ross 1966, cxxiv, has clearly identified this modern concept of "functional" as transeunt efficient causality for Aristotle: "[A]ction and passion involve a distinction between agent and patient. . . . Power is a capacity in A of producing a change in B. . . . This may be called transeunt δύναμις, inasmuch as two things are concerned."

15. Here *ergon* is clearly intrinsic and constitutive, linked with the preceding intrinsic *telos* and with the succeeding intrinsic *arche hoion psyche*. This part of the text contains no reference to the audience at all, and the *ergon* of a *psyche* is always intrinsic.

McKeon 1946, 198: "The criteria for the construction of the plot are to be found neither in the adequacy of the representation to what happens to be the case nor in the practical or moral responses of audiences, but in the structure which is achieved in the interplay of action, character, and thought pertinent to the poetic end."

Crane 1953, 52 f: "its distinctive synthesizing principle. That principle is what he calls . . . the peculiar *dynamis* or 'power' of the form—that which animates its parts and makes them one determinate whole, as the 'soul' is the most formal principle . . . of the living being . . . [so] Aristotle defines tragedy . . . [in] a formula which specifies not merely the three material components . . . but also the distinctive *dynamis* which is the actuality or form of their combination." 150: " '[T]he formal nature is of greater importance than the material nature' inasmuch as the 'form' of any individual object . . . is the principle or cause 'by reason of which the matter is some definite thing'."

16. This links the "achieving the katharsis" *(perainousa katharsin)* of the definition with the *mythos* as a whole, with its sequential causal structure, not merely with its end. The *telos* of the tragedy must be distinguished from the *teleuten* (the last part) of the *mythos*, from its resolution *(lysis)*. The *mythos is* the final cause of the tragedy, but it does not itself *have* a final cause.

Else 1957, 230, has made this clear: "Περαίνειν . . . has from its root (πέρας) the sense 'carry through, bring to completion' . . . emphasizing the duration . . . a process which goes forward throughout the play, rather than simply an end-result which accrues to the spectator." By contrast, Nehamas (Rorty 1992, 307), links *perainousa katharsin* with the end *(teleuten)* of the *mythos*: "catharsis . . . 'clarification' . . . 'resolution' or 'explanation' . . . clarification of the pitiful and fearful incidents of the drama itself . . . 'resolution', 'denouement' or 'solution' of the tragic plot, the *lysis*."

17. Commentators introduce multiple definitory *tele*, e.g., Lear (Rorty 1992, 328): "Aristotle . . . defines tragedy in part by the effect it has on its audience." This accords well with modern pluralistic thinking but not with Aristotle's hierarchical and definitory philosophizing. Nor does it accord with his overriding concern for the unity of the *mythos* and of the tragedy as a whole, which depends on there being only one definitory *telos*, one *arche* that "besouls" it. Cf. Crane 1953, 64.

Halper (Sim 1999, 222) has addressed the inner complexity of a tragedy and the need for all its constitutive parts to have unity. This permits only one definitory *telos*, the plot as formal-final cause: "Claims about the unity of tragedy's parts function normatively as well as descriptively... the more a tragedy is one, the better it is as a tragedy."

18. Here is the only textual disagreement between Kassel and Halliwell that bears on the argument. Kassel brackets 1450a17–20, Halliwell does not. Halliwell's argument is exegetical rather than textual. He reasons that since tragedy is *mimetic* of human life, its priority of action to agent mirrors a like priority in life. This argument runs counter to *Poetics* 8, which sharply contrasts the agent-focused structure of life with the action-focused one of art *(peri hena-peri mian praxin)*. And it runs counter to *E.N.*'s categorial priority of agent *(ho pratton)* to his actions *(praxeis)*, which are his accidents *(symbebekota)* and are inherently plural and derivative. For the agent is the *arche* and responsible cause *(aition)* of his actions, not the other way round. It is not an action as such that is good or bad but rather the way the agent does it, so that the human good does not lie in actions as such but rather in actions done as the practically wise man would do them (Halliwell 1987, 146–162 and 1995, 51).

Janko 1987, 86, also does not bracket and argues: "This is Aristotle's main argument for the primacy of plot. It depends on an analogy between actual human conduct and its representation. In life, people aim at an *END (telos)* that is an *ACTION.* . . . Since tragedy represents action and life, it must represent people acting to attain the end for man, happiness, which is itself an action. . . . Aristotle combines the perspective of the *Poetics* with that of the *Ethics* here." This argument, even more than Halliwell's, is incompatible with *Poetics* 8 and with *E.N.*

Cooper 1975, chapter II, has shown that *eudaimonia* is not an action but rather "a comprehensively inclusive second-order end" (133).

19. The five subordinate constitutive parts are matter or potentiality for the *mythos*, analogous to the body of an animal. Aristotle is here bringing his normal constitutive-causal analysis to bear, since otherwise the action-soul analogy would make no sense.

Gilson 1965, 179: "Everything that the artist submits to the form of his art belongs to the matter of the work."

Belfiore (Rorty 1992, 361 ff.) contrasts Aristotle's priority of plot with the modern priority of character: "While Aristotle believes plot to be of central importance in tragedy, modern concerns instead center on characterization and psychology... [for Aristotle] character is strictly secondary to plot, which alone is essential to tragedy... Aristotle's plot-centered view of tragedy...." 376, Note 25: "I argue for a strict interpretation of Aristotle's plot-character distinction, and against the tendency of many modern scholars to blur this distinction." Cf. Vernant (Rorty 1992, 37).

Janko 1987, 200, applies Aristotle's four causes to a tragedy in a way that has no basis in the text: "The material cause of a tragedy is paper and ink, or perhaps actors and their voices when it is performed *(SPECTACLE)*. Its formal causes are stated by Aristotle at 49 b 24, in his definition of tragedy.... Its efficient cause is the poet . . . or . . . the actors who perform it. Its final cause is its *END* or *FUNCTION*, the catharsis of the tragic emotions of the audience (49 b 27)."

20. Else 1957, 248: "Every detail of the six 'parts' is deduced . . . from the definition . . . the controlling factor is the word δρώντων." Cf. 570. I argue, by contrast, that the word *praxeos* is "the controlling factor." "In the manner of dramatic enactment" *(di' dronton)* and *praxeos* cannot mean the same, since they fall under different differentiae, *di' dronton* under manner of imitation *(hos)* and *praxeos* under objects of imitation *(ha)*. Moreover, in epic *praxeos* remains the controlling object of imitation, while *di' dronton* is replaced by "in the manner of narrative" *(di' apangelias)*. And Aristotle through his entire argument uses *mimesis praxeos* as his essential premise, never *di' dronton* or *di' apangelias*. Finally, if *di' dronton* were "the controlling factor," *opsis* should be the most, not the least, important of the six constitutive parts.

21. The analogous use of "to structure" *(synistanai)* in *Poetics* and in Aristotle's biological works strengthens the *mythos*-soul analogy and shows that his language is technical in both contexts. Halliwell 1986, 23, has well expressed the function of the action as constitutive formal-final cause in contrast to modern notions of structure. He recognizes the *mythos* as "both the organised design and the significant substance or content of the poem." Halper (Sim 1999, 221): "First, his claim that 'plot is principle and soul of tragedy' (1450a38–39) is not the throw-away comment it seemed: soul is the form of a body, and plot is the principle of tragedy in the sense that both are formal causes."

22. Halliwell 1987, 40. Golden and Harrison 1968, 123: "Aristotle's note thus differentiates between the parallel realms of art and nature. In nature, personality causes action. . . . In art, action . . . can thus be said to 'cause' character and thought." 128: "[I]n life character causes action, whereas in art action causes character."

23. Halliwell 1987, 42. But Belfiore 1992, 60: "The *ergon* of tragedy, unlike that of living things, has an external reference: tragedy arouses emotion in human beings."

24. There are differences of translation in chapters 11 and 13 that bear on the argument. Aristotle here uses *echein* as a synonym of *einai*, sometimes in the present and sometimes in the future tense (e.g., 1452b30–3a7). I therefore translate *echei* as "has" and *hexei* as "will have," so that pity or fear (or the pitiful or fearsome) are something the tragedy intrinsically has or will have as its objective emotive content, incorporated into its structure. He uses both *echein* and *einai* here but not *poiein*.

Halliwell 1987, 43 and Else 1957, 364 f., take *echein* as a synonym of *poiein*, "produce," so that pity or fear are an external transeuntly caused effect of the structure of the action, rather than its intrinsic emotive content. But this translation, while not impossible, is not the most natural. The text at this point is concerned with the intrinsic structure and qualitative nature *(poia)* of the *praxis* and makes no reference to the audience. Aristotle often uses the future indicative to mark a consequential relationship, e.g., in *An. Pr.* he uses it to designate the conclusion of a syllogism. It is "the finest recognition" *(kalliste de anagnorisis)*, which most successfully incorporates the specifically tragic emotive content into the *praxis* of a tragedy.

The translation "produce" would make the structural properties of a tragedy's *praxis* means to the production of an extrinsic emotional effect in the audience without any objectively emotive content intrinsic to the *praxis* itself. This would reduce the *praxis* to mere structure, rather than letting it function as a qualitative *(poion)* Aristotelian *eidos-telos*. The analogy with the soul of an animal would thereby be broken, and Aristotle's ontological and cognitive priority of the object to the subject would be reversed. If "the fearsome" is defined simply as "what produces fear," then that production itself and hence the audience's subjectively felt emotion become unintelligible. For the audience would experience fear of something that is not objectively fearful, and the cognitive dimension in human emotions would have no object. Hence I believe that translating *echein* as a synonym of *einai* rather than of *poiein* is more in accord with the text.

25. Else 1957, 379–385, argues that recognition *(anagnorisis)* of a person as kin implies a preceding failure of recognition, a mistake or error *(hamartia)*. For *anagnorisis*, which is part of the action, occurs at a definite time in it, so that up to that time there must have been *hamartia*. *Hamartia* is used as a synonym of *agnoia*, and both are given a causal function *(di' hamartian*; 13.1453a9–10; 15–16 and *di' agnoian*; 14.1453b35).

26. The reluctance to draw the normal Aristotelian implications of the analogy shows itself in giving the action of a tragedy an extrinsic transeuntly efficient causal function (see Note 14 above), rather than the intrinsic causally constitutive function of an animal's soul. But many commentators take the analogy itself seriously at this point in the text, though they do not remain consistent with it. Cf. Else 1957, 242 f: "The μῦθος is the imitation of the action, says Aristotle; he means it in the same sense that a man's soul is the man. For the plot is the *structure* of the play, around which the material 'parts' are laid, just as the soul is the structure of a man. It is well known that in Aristotle's biology the soul— i.e., the form—is 'prior' to the body; and we shall see that he thinks of the plot as prior to the poem in exactly the same way." Cf. also Freeland (Rorty 1992, 119).

27. This preference sometimes shows itself in the use of different translations for the same word *telos*, even by the same author. E.g., function, end, purpose, object, final cause, aim, goal. Cf. Janko 1987, 217: "[P]lot amounts to the *END* of tragedy, that by means of which it performs its *FUNCTION*." But Aristotle never calls a mere means a *telos*.

28. Halliwell 1986, 27, speaks of "the relative independence of poetry" and argues, 1987, 131: "Ar.'s theory cannot allow plot-structure and the tragic effect to be treated as distinct issues." 91: "To anyone who argued that it is a mistake to confuse a poetic work with its emotional effects, Ar. would respond that the understanding of kinds of poetry, as of kinds of reality, cannot but involve us in judgments on their emotional power." Cf. Halliwell (Rorty 1992, 255 f.): "[T]he *telos* and *ergon* of tragedy must incorporate pleasure . . . the end or function of tragedy is not . . . some single, discrete factor . . . 'what, on Aristotle's reckoning, is poetry for?' . . . 'for its own sake' in the sense that its aims are not directly instrumental to some externally specifiable goal . . . 'what is poetry for?' . . . aesthetic experience." Cf. also Rorty (Rorty 1992, 2), who speaks of the "various

aims" of the poetic arts, which include the *hetero-telic* one of "bringing us to some sort of recognition." Rorty, like Halliwell, does not recognize the categorial priority of *ousia* to *pros ti* and thereby the categorial incompatibility of *auto-telic* and *hetero-telic* definitions. Neither *argues,* however, that the Aristotelian categories with their *pros˘hen* structure are irrelevant to the *Poetics.*

29. Woodruff (Rorty 1992, 84) formulates the problem neatly: "A product of mimesis is a thing in its own right, but it is also *of* something else." Else 1957, 322, sees the *poietes-mimetes* conjunction as paradoxical: "A poet, then, is an *imitator* in so far as he is a *maker,* viz. of plots. The paradox is obvious. Aristotle has . . . the bearing of a concept which originally meant a faithful *copying* of preexistent things, to make it mean a *creation* of things. . . . Copying is after the fact; Aristotle's μίμησις creates the fact." Kandinsky's (Lindsay and Vergo 1994, 832) solution is to transform the representational content, which is what Aristotle also does: "In every more or less naturalistic work a portion of the already existing world is taken (man, animal, flower, guitar, pipe . . .) and is transformed under the yoke of the various means of expression in the artistic sense. A linear and painterly 'reformulation' of the 'subject'."

30. Else 1957, 575: "[T]he poet is free to play fast and loose with chronology."

31. McKeon (Crane 1952, 162): "Art imitates nature; the form joined to matter in the physical world is the same form that is expressed in the matter of the art."

32. Halliwell 1986, 135: "[T]he poet is not to be tied to transcribing reality in any straightforward manner . . . fashion and structure it in accordance with the requirements of his art." Cf. Blundell (Rorty 1992, 159): "change in focus from attributes of (dramatic) persons to attributes of plays . . . parts of a play are not parts of a person." Also Else 1957, 244, recognizes that *ethe* and *dianoia* are technical terms in the *Poetics*: "character and thought . . . technical meanings which the two words are to have as 'parts' of tragedy—a status which is not necessarily the same as they have in life." I would only suggest a slight change in word order from "not necessarily" to "necessarily not." Else, 586 f., also contrasts the principles of composition of history, of art, and of life: "the explicit contrast . . . between μία πρᾶξις and εἰς χρόνος as principles of composition."

33. This omission is indeed startling, as is Aristotle's disjoining and rank-ordering of *praxis, ethe,* and *dianoia.* He argues in *Poetics* 6 that *praxis* implies a doer *(pratton),* but then selectively allows only *ethe* and *dianoia* as objects of imitation that are implied by *praxis.* Frede (Rorty 1992, 211): "In tragedy we do not have the moral philosopher's hypothetical sovereign agent."

34. See Note 18 above. Halliwell 1986, 149: "*Poetics* . . . action and character analytically separated, together with a statement of the possibility of tragedies which dispense with character altogether . . . difficult to reconcile with the close link between action and character which I have attributed to Aristotle."

35. Halliwell 1986, 106: "[O]n Aristotle's own admission elsewhere, necessity plays little part in the sphere of human action. . . . But necessity stands for an extreme or ideal of unity . . . overstating the requirement of unity of action." Cf. Halliwell 1987, 107. Butcher 1951, 166, recognizes "necessity" as art-specific: " 'The

rule of probability' as also that of 'necessity', refers rather to the internal structure of a poem; it is the inner law which secures the cohesion of the parts."

Chapter 4. *Agent-Centering, Patient-Centering, Object-Centering*

1. Rorty (Rorty 1992, 2 f.): "Because they are representational, all the poetic arts include, among their various aims, that of bringing us to some sort of recognition . . . the best effects of tragic drama derive from its representational truthfulness." 8: "[D]rama reveals the unified structure of a life." Cf. Halliwell 1986, 157. Against this, Halper (Sim 1999, 225): "Yet, though tragedy imitates human actions, its genus is not actions but imitation. As an imitation, tragic action, that is, plot, is wholly different from the action it imitates."

2. Rorty (Rorty 1992, 17): "Tragedies. . . . Like well-formed rhetoric, they promote a sense of shared civic life, and like rhetoric, they do so both emotionally and cognitively." Lear (Rorty 1992, 332), argues that poetry is not rhetoric because it does not try to persuade its audience but only aims to produce an emotional response. This, however, takes no cognizance of the fact that rhetoric also aims to produce an emotional response. More importantly, what matters is not *what* is produced in an audience (persuasion or emotion), but rather *that* something is produced, which functions as definitory *telos*. Other scholars have argued against the subsumption of poetry under rhetoric. Halliwell 1986, 298 f., speaks of "the rhetorical bias of criticism." And McKeon (Crane 1952, 171) argues: "[W]hat later writers learned from Aristotle applicable to literature, they derived from the *Rhetoric* rather than from the *Poetics*. . . . Yet that change marks them as significantly different from Aristotle, since to confuse rhetoric and poetics would in his system be a Platonizing error. He, himself, distinguished the two disciplines sharply."

3. The title of a recent book by Harris 1999, *Agent-Centered Morality,* is based on Aristotle's ethics, which Harris sees as agent-centered in contrast to the Enlightenment's act-centered moral perspective.

4. Polansky (Preus and Anton 1992, 211–225) notes that Aristotle is untroubled by the difficulties of how temporal successiveness and having parts can be excluded from *energeiai,* how they can be conceived as if they were simples. Perhaps Cooper 1975, 105, solves this problem by characterizing the ethical nature of an action adverbially as a "style," which is indeed much like a simple. And Kosman (Rorty 1980, 114) emphasizes the derivativeness of ethical actions from ethical agents, so that *eu* is indeed much like a simple.

5. Sparshott 1994, 318.

6. This straight line is different from that which represents patient-centering. The incompatibility of ethical and tragic action has been recognized by scholars. Bittner (Rorty 1992, 105–108): "According to Aristotle's *Ethics*, moral excellence is located primarily in character traits, only derivatively in actions. . . . But then why does the *Poetics* not allow, indeed recommend, plays centered on character rather than an action? . . . Aristotle is arguing that this compression of all the happiness and unhappiness of the agent into what is being decided now requires

centering the play on one action." Cf. Halliwell 1986, 206 f: "The relation in the Aristotelian moral system between *eudaimonia* and *eutuchia* is that of the essential and primary to the subordinate and secondary... *Poetics* ... accentuation on the *eutuchia-dustuchia* dichotomy ... Aristotle's theory commits tragedy to an engagement not directly with the ethical centre of happiness, but with the external conditions." 234: "*[Poetics]* centres around the changes in men's external states, rather than their virtues and vices."

7. Consensus is not likely to be reached. Perhaps Irwin (Sherman 1999, 10) puts it best: "The virtuous but unlucky person is not happy; the lucky but nonvirtuous person is unhappy."

8. That is why Aristotle says that a man and a picture of a man are called man *homonymously*, *Cat.* 1. They have only the name in common, but different definitions. Cf. Anton 1996, 72 ff: "[I]n order to supply examples of *homonyma legomena*, which name *ousiai*, Aristotle had to select his instances from two distinct domains of existence, i.e., from incommensurate types ... the logic of Aristotle's categorial theory demanded that his examples of *homonyma* came not from items that fall within different genera of being, viz. *ousia* and, say, quality, but items denoted by the genus *ousia* only. The other domain of existence that could qualify to meet this condition is clearly that of *techne:* the artifacts *qua* substances.... The problem is not so much whether we can speak of portraits and engines as cases of *ousia*, but rather whether they have the ontological status of individual entities and not of accidents.... The fact remains that though such things are not by nature *(physei)*, but are brought about by art *(apo technes)*, Aristotle's philosophy allows for the possibility of treating them as cases of *ousia* ... in some special sense, and hence nonreducible to accidental beings ... artifacts are not reducible to accidental properties ... the ontological status of things brought about by art is in a serious sense that of *ousia*.... Aristotle insists that the artist is an efficient cause, and *qua* τεχνίτης he imparts to his selected materials the *eidos* or final cause appropriate to it. Aristotle is convinced of the naturalness of *techne*. Hence, in so far as individual things by *techne* are cases of *ousia* they are *loci* of properties. The fact that Aristotle uses the term *ousia* in the opening passage of the *Categories* for both domains of existence, is indicative that he held this view.... Since portraits are not things that are said to be in a subject, they are included in the genus *ousia*."

9. Engberg-Pedersen (Rorty 1996, 126): "those addressed in a rhetorical performance." By contrast, Heath 1996, xix: "A tragedy is a poem, not a performance."

10. McKeon (Crane 1952, 173): "But the natural center of gravity in rhetoric is the audience." Golden 1992, 89, locates "the essence of tragedy" in audience response. The triangular analysis is applied to poetry by modern critics, though never by Aristotle. Stead 1967, 11: "A poem may be said to exist in a triangle, the points of which are, first, the poet, second, his audience, and third, that area of experience which we call variously 'Reality', 'Truth', or 'Nature'."

11. The most systematic challenge to my characterization of rhetorical action as patient-centered, and hence in the category of *pros ti*, comes from Garver

1994, 74, who sees rhetoric as a practical, not a productive art. He places it into the category of *ousia:* "Since a speech is a substance made of form and matter" (40).

Garver's analysis conflates *praxis* and *techne* or *poiesis*, on whose strict separation in *E.N.* VI. 4 and *Met.* IX. 6 my analysis depends. I accord rhetorical action and its analogue, medical treatment, only instrumental value, while Garver accords them also inherent value, 32: "The essence of the rhetorical art is not winning, but arguing." Cooper 1975, chapter I, distinguishes *praxis* and *techne* or *poiesis* sharply.

12. Aristotle vacillates between accepting and rejecting rhetoric as a *techne* in his normal honorific sense, partly because a *bona fide techne* has a distinctive subject matter of its own while rhetoric can create persuasion in any subject matter, partly because some of the means of persuasion are reputable (e.g., *enthymeme*) while others may not be (e.g., *ethos, pathos, lexis*). He is, however, clear that if rhetoric employed only reputable means and hence became *epistemic*, its own distinctive nature would be destroyed (*Rhetoric* III. 14.1415a38–b7; I. 4.1359b2–18).

The priority of audience response is well expressed as "controls" by Fortenbaugh 1975, 19, who however extends it to poetry: "Tragedy was associated with two emotions which were recognized not only as intelligent and reasonable responses but also as important controls in determining the kinds of actions depicted in tragic poetry."

The distinction between rhetoric and teaching based on *episteme* has been acknowledged. Irwin (Rorty 1996, 143): "Aristotle discusses persuasion rather than truth." Engberg-Pedersen (Rorty 1996, 129): "The scientist will go for the 'first principles' *(archai)*, the orator for what is convincing to his audience."

13. Irwin (Rorty 1996, 148): "The *Rhetoric*, like the *Topics*, is meant to equip us for 'encounters with the many', but, unlike the *Topics*, says nothing about 'redirecting' *(metabibazein)* the views of the many. The aim of redirecting the views of the many is part of Aristotle's conception of ethical argument."

14. Halliwell 1986, 289: "In contrast to Aristotle, for whom rhetoric is one component element within tragedy and epic, and for whom the poetic production of emotion is not a matter of manipulating an audience but of constructing a literary artefact with certain objectively emotive properties . . . the Hellenistic age saw the establishment of a thoroughly rhetorical view of poetry."

For a compact overview, see Halliwell (Rorty 1992, 409–424). See also McKeon 1946 and McKeon (Crane 1952, 147–175).

Conclusion

1. There are many sorts of obscurantism in theory of art, which particularly seems to attract them. One familiar to, and rejected by, Aristotle is the Platonic notion of divine inspiration as a sort of madness. Aristotle prefers his *technites* in any *techne* to be sane and rationally in control. One rather funny sort of obscurantism is an undifferentiated flood of words without distinction be-

tween what is art-specific and what is not, what is essential and what is not, what is objective and what is subjective. The most prevalent sort, however, is reductionism, which means explaining art in terms that are not art-specific.

2. Kandinsky (Lindsay and Vergo 1994).

3. Kandinsky (Lindsay and Vergo 1994, 821): "Concrete painting offers a kind of parallel with symphonic music by possessing a purely artistic content. Purely pictorial means are alone responsible for this content. From this *exclusive responsibility* arises the necessity for the *perfect accuracy* of the composition from the point of view of balance (values, weights of forms, and of color-masses, etc.) and for the perfect accuracy of every part of the composition, *to the least little detail*, since inaccuracies cannot be concealed. . . . This is artistic mathematics, the opposite of the mathematics of science."

4. Kandinsky (Lindsay and Vergo 1994, 173 f.). 658 f: "indicate that efforts to derive art from geographical, economic, political, or other purely 'positive' factors can never be exhaustive, and that such methods cannot be free from bias . . . 'positive' factors play a subordinate role."

5. Kandinsky (Lindsay and Vergo 1994, 114–215).

Appendix

1. Nehamas (Rorty 1992, 313, Note 39).

2. Cooper 1963, 35.

3. Else 1957, 538.

4. Halliwell 1986, 103.

5. Kosman (Rorty 1992, 67 f.).

6. Halliwell 1986, 101.

7. Janko (Rorty 1992, 345).

8. Halliwell 1986, 102.

9. Butcher 1951, 209.

10. Frede (Rorty 1992, 197–219).

11. Nussbaum (Rorty 1992, 261–290).

12. Halliwell 1986, Translation and Commentary to *Poetics* 8.

13. Lear (Rorty 1992, 328).

14. The principle of charity, as I have used it, appears to be shared as an exegetical device by Sorabji (Rorty 1980, 202): "[T]here is an onus of proof on the interpreter who says that Aristotle is contradicting his official account." See also Wiggins (Rorty 1980, 223).

REFERENCES

Only books and articles cited in the Notes by author's name and date of publication are listed.

Anton, J. P. 1993. "Nietzsche's Critique of Aristotle's Theory of Tragic Emotions." In *Tragedy and Philosophy*, ed. N. Georgopoulos. New York: St. Martin's Press.

———. 1996. *Categories and Experience*. Binghamton, N.Y.: Dowling College Press.

Belfiore, E. 1992. *Tragic Pleasures*. Princeton: Princeton University Press.

———. 1992. "Aristotle and Iphigenia." In Rorty 1992.

Bittner, R. 1992. "One Action." In Rorty 1992.

Blundell, N. W. 1992. "Ethos and Dianoia Reconsidered." In Rorty 1992.

Booth, W. 1992. "The *Poetics* for a Practical Critic." In Rorty 1992.

Butcher, S. H., tr. 1951. *Aristotle's Theory of Poetry and Fine Art*. New York: Dover.

Code, A. 1984. "The Aporematic Approach to Primary Being in *Metaphysics* Z," *Canadian Journal of Philosophy* (Supp. 10).

Cooper, J. M. 1975. *Reason and Human Good in Aristotle*. Cambridge, Mass., London: Harvard University Press.

Cooper, L. 1963. *The Poetics of Aristotle: Its Meaning and Influence*. New York: Cooper Square Publishers.

Cleary, J. 1988. *Aristotle on the Many Senses of Priority*. Carbondale, Ill.: Southern Illinois University Press.

Crane, R. S. 1953. *The Languages of Criticism and the Structure of Poetry*. Toronto: University of Toronto Press.

———, ed. 1952. *Critics and Criticism*. Chicago: University of Chicago Press.

Düring, I., and G. E. L. Owen, eds. 1960. *Aristotle and Plato in the Mid-Fourth Century*. Göteborg: Elanders Boktryckeri Aktiebolag.

Else, G. F. 1957. *Aristotle's Poetics: The Argument*. Cambridge, Mass.: Harvard University Press.

Engberg-Pedersen, T. 1996. "Is there an Ethical Dimension to Aristotelian Rhetoric?" In Rorty 1996.

Fortenbaugh, W. W. 1975. *Aristotle on Emotion.* London: Duckworth.

Frede, D. 1992. "Necessity, Chance, and 'What Happens for the Most Part' in Aristotle's *Poetics.*" In Rorty 1992.

Freeland, C. A. 1992. "Plot Imitates Action." In Rorty 1992.

Furth, M. 1974. "Elements of Eleatic Ontology." In *The Pre-Socratics,* ed. A. P. D. Mourelatos. Garden City, N.Y.: Doubleday.

Garver, E. 1994. *Aristotle's Rhetoric: An Art of Character.* Chicago, London: University of Chicago Press.

Georgiadis, C. 1978. "Aristotle's Perspectives on Human Technical Work," *Dialectics and Humanism* (no. 3).

Gill, M. L. 1989. *Aristotle on Substance.* Princeton: Princeton University Press.

Gilson, E. 1965. *The Arts of the Beautiful.* New York: Scribners.

Golden, L. 1992. *Aristotle on Tragic and Comic Mimesis.* Atlanta: Scholars Press.

Golden, L., and O. B. Harrison, trs. 1968. *Aristotle's Poetics.* Englewood Cliffs, N. J.: Prentice-Hall.

Gould, T. 1990. *The Ancient Quarrel Between Poetry and Philosophy.* Princeton: Princeton University Press.

Grube, G. M. A., tr. 1958. *Aristotle on Poetry and Style.* Indianapolis: Hackett.

Halliwell, S., tr. 1987. *The Poetics of Aristotle* (Translation and Commentary). Chapel Hill, N. C.: University of North Carolina Press.

————. 1986. *Aristotle's Poetics.* Chicago: University of Chicago Press.

————. 1992. "Pleasure, Understanding, and Emotion" and "Epilogue." In Rorty 1992.

————, tr. 1995. *Aristotle's Poetics* (Loeb Classical Library). Cambridge, Mass., London: Harvard University Press.

Halper, E. 1999. "Poetry, History, and Dialectic." In Sim 1999.

Harris, G. W. 1999. *Agent-Centered Morality.* Berkeley, Los Angeles, London: University of California Press.

Hartmann, N. 1966. *Ästhetik.* Berlin: de Gruyter.

Heath, N., tr. 1996. *Aristotle: Poetics.* London: Penguin.

Husain, M. 1981. "The Multiplicity in Unity of Being *qua* Being in Aristotle's *pros hen* Equivocity," *New Scholasticism* (LV) 2.

————. 1992. "Aristotle's Wooden Statue of Hermes," *The Brock Review* (I) 1.

Irwin, T. 1996. "Ethics in the *Rhetoric* and in the *Ethics.*" In Rorty 1996.

————. 1999. "Permanent Happiness: Aristotle and Solon." In Sherman 1999.

Janko, R., tr. 1987. *Aristotle's Poetics.* Indianapolis, Cambridge: Hackett.

————. 1992. "From Catharsis to the Aristotelian Mean." In Rorty 1992.

Kandinsky, W. 1994. *Complete Writings on Art*, eds. K. C. Lindsay and P. Vergo. New York: Da Capo Press.

Kassel, R., ed. 1965. *Aristotelis De Arte Poetica Liber* (Oxford Classical Texts). Oxford: Oxford University Press.

Katayama, E. 1999. *Aristotle on Artifacts*. Albany: State University of New York Press.

Kosman, L. A. 1987. "Animals and other beings in Aristotle." In *Philosophical Issues in Aristotle's Biology*, eds. A. Gotthelf and J. G. Lennox. Cambridge, Mass.: Cambridge University Press.

———. 1992. "Acting: Drama as the Mimesis of Praxis." In Rorty 1992.

———. 1980. "Being Properly Affected: Virtues and Feelings in Aristotle's Ethics." In Rorty 1980.

Lear, J. 1992. "Katharsis." In Rorty 1992.

Lucas, D. W. 1968. *Aristotle's Poetics* (Introduction, Commentary, Appendices). Oxford: Clarendon Press.

McKeon, R. 1946 and 1947. "Aristotle's Conception of Language and the Arts of Language," *Classical Philology* (XLI) no 4 and (XLII) no. 1.

———. 1952. "Literary Criticism and the Concept of Imitation in Antiquity." In Crane 1952.

———. 1965. "Rhetoric and Poetic in the Philosophy of Aristotle." In *Aristotle's Poetics and English Literature*, ed. E. Olson. Chicago: University of Chicago Press.

Nehamas, A. 1992. "Pity and Fear in the *Rhetoric* and the *Poetics*." In Rorty 1992.

Nussbaum, M. C. 1986. *The Fragility of Goodness*. New York: Cambridge University Press.

———. 1992. "Tragedy and Self-Sufficiency: Plato and Aristotle on Fear and Pity." In Rorty 1992.

Owen, G. E. L. 1960. "Logic and Metaphysics in Some Earlier Works of Aristotle." In Düring and Owen 1960.

Owens, J. 1981. "Aristotle—Teacher of Those Who Know" and "Aristotle—Cognition a Way of Being." In *Aristotle: The Collected Papers of Joseph Owens*, ed. J. R. Catan. Albany: State University of New York Press.

Polansky, R. 1992. "*Energeia* in Aristotle's *Metaphysics* IX." In Preus and Anton 1992.

Preus, A., and J. P. Anton, eds. 1992. *Aristotle's Ontology*. Albany: State University of New York Press.

Race, W. H. Unpublished Manuscript. "Elements of Plot in Pindar."

Reeve, C. D. C. 2000. *Substantial Knowledge*. Indianapolis, London: Hackett Publishing Company.

Rorty, A. O. 1992. "The Psychology of Aristotelian Tragedy." In *Essays on Aristotle's Poetics*, ed. A. O. Rorty. Princeton: Princeton University Press.

138

————, ed. 1996. *Essays on Aristotle's Rhetoric.* Berkeley, Los Angeles, London: University of California Press.

————, ed. 1980. *Essays on Aristotle's Ethics.* Berkeley, Los Angeles, London: University of California Press.

Ross, W. D., ed. 1966 (first edition 1924). *Aristotle's Metaphysics.* Oxford: Clarendon Press.

Sim, M., ed. 1995. *Crossroads of Norm and Nature.* Lanham, London: Rowman and Littlefield.

Smith, R. 1992. "Filling in Nature's Deficiencies." In Preus and Anton 1992.

Sorabji, R. 1980. "Aristotle on the Role of Intellect." In Rorty 1980.

Sparshott, F. 1982. *The Theory of the Arts.* Princeton: Princeton University Press.

————. 1994. *Taking Life Seriously.* Toronto: University of Toronto Press.

Stead, C. K., ed. 1967. *The New Poetic.* London: Penguin.

Vernant, J.-P. 1992. "Myth and Tragedy." In Rorty 1992.

Wians, W. 1992. "Saving Aristotle from Nussbaum's *Phainomena.*" In Preus and Anton 1992.

Wiggins, D. 1980. "Deliberation and Practical Reason." In Rorty 1980.

Woodruff, P. 1992. "Aristotle on Mimesis." In Rorty 1992.

Index of Names

SUBJECT INDEX

The *Subject Index* lists all terms in English. If a term occurs in the text in transliterated Greek, it is added to the English term in parentheses. If a term occurs in the text also in Greek script, it is so added in parentheses.

INDEX OF PASSAGES CITED

R 555